Other Books by Mark Goldblatt

Africa Speaks (2002)
Sloth (2010)
Bumper Stick Liberalism (2012)
Twerp (2013)
The Unrequited (2013)
Finding the Worm (2015)
Right Tool for the Job: A Memoir of Manly Concerns (2017)

I Feel, Therefore I Am

The Triumph of Woke Subjectivism

Mark Goldblatt

Published by Bombardier Books
An Imprint of Post Hill Press
ISBN: 978-1-63758-285-5
ISBN (eBook): 978-1-63758-286-2

I Feel, Therefore I Am:
The Triumph of Woke Subjectivism
© 2022 by Mark Goldblatt
All Rights Reserved

Cover Design by Tiffani Shea

No part of this book may be reproduced, stored in a retrieval system, or transmitted by any means without the written permission of the author and publisher.

Post Hill Press
New York • Nashville
posthillpress.com

Published in the United States of America
1 2 3 4 5 6 7 8 9 10

"In all this I feel a grave danger, the danger of what might be called cosmic impiety. The concept of 'truth' as something dependent upon facts largely outside human control has been one of the ways in which philosophy hitherto has inculcated the necessary element of humility. When this check upon pride is removed, a further step is taken on the road towards a certain kind of madness—the intoxication of power.... I am persuaded that this intoxication is the greatest danger of our time, and that any philosophy which, however unintentionally, contributes to it is increasing the danger of vast social disaster."

—Bertrand Russell, 1945,
A History of Western Philosophy

"We shall soon be in a world in which a man may be howled down for saying that two and two make four, in which furious party cries will be raised against anybody who says that cows have horns, in which people will persecute the heresy of calling a triangle a three-sided figure, and hang a man for maddening a mob with the news that grass is green."

—G. K. Chesterton, 1926,
"On Modern Controversy"

CONTENTS

INTRODUCTION

Our Pontius Pilate Moment

The trial of Jesus, whether you take it as historical account or literary artifact, is one of the signature narratives of Western civilization. According to John's Gospel, Jewish leaders arrest Jesus and bring him to the Roman governor of Judea, hoping Pilate will rid them of the man who proclaims himself the Son of God.

Pilate, however, doesn't want to get involved in a Jewish matter. When the leaders persist, Pilate agrees to interrogate the prisoner. He asks Jesus if he is the king of the Jews. Jesus answers that his kingdom is not of this world. "You *are* a king then!" Pilate says. To which Jesus replies, "You say I am a king. In fact, the reason I was born and came into the world is to testify to the truth. Everyone on the side of truth listens to me."

Pilate listens to Jesus's reply and then asks, "What is truth?"

It's the most sinister question in the Bible. Pilate walks off, however, before Jesus can reply.

The fact that he exits is critical. It tells us what's going on in Pilate's mind. When he asks, "What is truth?" he is not requesting that Jesus elaborate on that other kingdom over which he claims dominion. Nor is he inquiring, in a philosophical way, what it means to say that something is true. Rather, Pilate is dismissing the entire notion of truth. He is, in effect, rolling his eyes at the unsophisticated, even vulgar, notion that truth matters in some abstract, transcendental sense.

What matters, from his standpoint, is power. If you've got it, here and now, you get to decide what's true. Pilate has the power to put Jesus to death or dismiss the charges against him. Power is Pilate's truth. It's what he knows, what he feels with every fiber of his being. (Which is the reason Friedrich Nietzsche, who had a thing for bully boys, called Pilate the "solitary figure worthy of honor" in the New Testament.[1]) It's what has gotten him where he is and what will get him where he wants to go.

Weaklings argue about truth. Those with power grow their own.

America, circa 2022, is having a Pontius Pilate moment. What is truth? Whatever you will. Whatever you can. Whatever you *dare*. Truth is what you have the power to make true; if you're calling the shots, you get to decide. Everyone else can pound dirt.

You think you've got a handle on what's true? Maybe you do. This week. Next week, though, the winds of power will shift, and what's true will shift too. Remember when men were male? When women were female? When equal rights were fair? When history was what happened? When facts were nonnegotiable? When due process assigned the burden of proof to the accuser? When logic and evidence decided the outcome of arguments?

That was last week.

If truth is a function of power, and power comes and goes, you can no longer say what *is* true, objectively. You can say only what *feels* true, subjectively. For the time being. Does the earth revolve around the sun? Astronomical observations point in that direction, and at the moment, the powers-that-be stand behind those astronomical observations. But the powers-that-be didn't always line up behind astronomy. (Ask Galileo.) Plus, it sure *feels* as though the sun is doing laps around the earth.

The proposition that the earth revolves around the sun must therefore be interrogated! It must be *deconstructed*! Who collected those astronomical observations? Who empowered them to do so? What stake did they have in the conclusion? Doesn't a conclusion based on astronomical observations privilege a specific Enlightenment view of the earth as an inanimate body hurtling through space rather than as a living, nurturing mother figure, teeming with flesh and blood creatures as well as mischievous spirits and ancient gods—as many communities of color have long believed? Doesn't astronomy, in short, reinscribe the cultural hegemony of Europeans over communities of color?

That seems not only racist but pretty damn ironic since, by the reckoning of several prominent Enlightenment thinkers, perception creates reality. Thus, the sun wouldn't even exist if it were not continuously being perceived by creatures capable of perception. But if the sun wouldn't exist without being perceived, and creatures capable of perception are found, as far as we know, only on earth, isn't it equally true, and perhaps even more true, to say that the sun revolves around the earth?

The proposition that the earth revolves around the sun is therefore freighted with power dynamics. It fits a dominant narrative constructed relatively recently by white male Europeans that ranks their feelings over the feelings of people of color, millions upon millions of them, who lived and died convinced that the sun revolved around the earth. They had one narrative. Europeans have a different one. Right now, as you read these words, the European narrative is dominant. Neither narrative, however, is objectively truer than the other.

Suppose, however, we don't follow Pilate's lead. Suppose we don't roll our eyes and exit stage left. Suppose we *do* ask the philosophical question: What is truth? The traditional answer is that truth is a correspondence between what's thought or said and a reality that exists independently of what's thought or said. When you say something that corresponds with reality, you are saying something true. "The earth revolves around the sun," from that traditional perspective, is a true statement. "John Lennon was a member of the Beatles" is also a true statement. So is, "Columbus sailed the ocean blue in fourteen hundred and ninety-two."

In every true statement, you have two partners: the statement and reality. But reality is the senior partner. It calls the tune. You need to adjust your statements to reality since the other way won't work; reality won't adjust itself to you. It *can't* adjust itself to you because it's not a conscious thing; it doesn't care. It just is. Which is the reason you want to take a cold, hard look at reality before you start to cough up truth claims.

That's the correspondence theory of truth. It's the traditional answer to the question, "What is truth?" But of course it raises a related question: "What is reality?" According to the science fiction writer Philip K. Dick, "Reality is that which, when you stop believing in it, doesn't go away."[2] It's a good definition. It's common sense but with an ironic flourish. The standard definition is more prosaic but says the same thing: reality is that which exists independently of the thought processes of a thinker. Reality, in other words, is what's out there, beyond the workings of our minds. It includes us, we're a part of it, but it doesn't depend on us. It is what it is. It is what it is, moreover, whether we like it or not. It exists regardless of our feelings about it, our rooting interests in it, our notions of what and how it should be.

Does correspondence make truth? Or does power make truth?

That's the intellectual and sociopolitical schism rumbling American culture at the moment. It's a struggle over the nature of truth. From the power-makes-truth side of the schism, it feels natural to award a Pulitzer Prize to a *New York Times* journalist for her ideologically slanted revisionist history of the United States, despite her assertion that the project "explicitly denies objectivity." From the correspondence-makes-truth side, however, the entire point of revising a popular view of history is for the new account to be more objectively true, more in correspondence with reality, than the previous one. That complaint will fall on deaf ears at the *New York Times*, however: "We stated in the intro this was a reframing of history.... The fight here is about who gets to control the national narrative, and therefore, the nation's shared memory of itself."

How, then, should those on the correspondence side react when the project becomes required reading in public school history classes across the country? Are they supposed to shrug and say, "The truth will out!" But what does that mean in this context? Their opponents believe that power creates truth. So even if the project's central claims do not correspond with reality, if a sufficient number of readers with a sufficient share of power are convinced by them, those claims will become true.

It's not just history that's up for grabs. It's justice. Without a consensus on the nature of truth, how do you determine just outcomes? (It's a point that would not be lost on Pilate.) What happens when a nominee for the Supreme Court is accused of sexual assault...back when he was in high school? Should he be confirmed? You've got powerful interests on both sides. You've also got the reality of what happened three decades earlier. What determines the truth of the accusations, correspondence or power? Does it matter that the only three witnesses named by the accuser deny they were present, or that the accuser cannot produce a shred of objectively verifiable evidence that she and the nominee have ever been in the same place at the same time? Or is that irrelevant because you *know* the accusations are true; you *feel* their truth in your bones? Does the fact that the nominee is eventually confirmed, that his political supporters are powerful enough to get him on the court, prove that the accusations are false? Or does the fact that more Americans believe her than him, and that the truth of the accusations is now routinely asserted by powerful voices in politics, academia, and the media prove that the accusations are true?

What is a just outcome?

What is justice?

The answer depends on what truth is.

As I write these words, it is no longer a truth universally acknowledged that if your aunt had balls, she'd be your uncle. Nothing *in reality* has changed. *In reality*, self-identified aunts who have balls are still uncles. The fact that this particular truth is no longer universally acknowledged tells us that many Americans no longer feel constrained, in their truth judgments, by reality.

You can understand it, on one level. It's a democratic impulse. *Who are you to tell me what's true? Who gave you that power?* The response, from the correspondence-makes-truth side, is that there's no democracy of truth, no majority rule. If there were such a thing as majority rule over truth, we could solve the problem of global warming simply by convincing a sufficient number of people that it's not a real problem.

But that's not how reality works. If global warming is true, it's true even if a steady majority says otherwise.

So, too, from the correspondence-makes-truth side, *if your aunt has balls, she's your uncle*. Even if every cable news talking head, gender studies professor, and guru in drag[3] says otherwise.

Which brings us to Caitlyn (née Bruce) Jenner. Olympic gold medalist in the decathlon. Reality TV star. Wildly successful entrepreneur. Caitlyn seems, on the basis of what is publicly known, a lovely fellow. But he has a reality problem. He *feels* like a woman. That's not the problem. He *identifies* as a woman. Still not a problem. Therefore, he insists, he *is* a woman. That's the problem. He isn't. Not in reality and thus not from a correspondence-makes-truth perspective. He isn't a woman, not even if he plays one on TV, not even if every man, woman, child, and viewer demographic agrees to pretend that he is. Reality doesn't care what Caitlyn feels, or how sincere his feelings are, or how he defines himself, or whether the rest of us play along. Caitlyn was born with balls. Ergo, he's a man. He's reportedly had his balls surgically removed. Doesn't matter. He's still a man. He is an adult male human being. The guy's a dude. Dude-hood is literally coded into his DNA.[4]

Critical Race Theory. The Me Too movement. Transgender-recognition. The controversies over each of these developments boil down to whether we think truth is a function of power or a correspondence with reality. How do we know what's true? Is it a subjective judgment imposed on us by institutions and experts empowered by the government, universities, and the media? Or is it an objective judgment, verifiable whenever the demand arises by direct observation and reproducible results?

The controversies over CRT, Me Too, and transgender-recognition are also, however, debates over individual and collective rights. What natural rights are due me because I am a person? What special rights can I claim because of wrongs done to my ancestors? To what degree are other persons, each with their own set of rights, compelled to acknowledge and respect my self-perception and system of beliefs?

To speak of such matters is necessarily to invoke the vocabulary and values of the European Enlightenment of the seventeenth and eighteenth centuries: rational inquiry, socioreligious tolerance, and inalienable rights. This kind of discourse may strike some readers today as "Eurocentric." But it is unavoidable. The vocabulary and values of the Enlightenment have become the magnetic north of the world's moral compass. Whenever a person, a community, or a nation feels aggrieved, their appeal to the conscience of humanity invokes reason, tolerance, or rights...even if their own cultures and traditions have not embraced those values. The common ground of reason, the peaceable default of tolerance, and the universality of basic rights are the starting points for debating individual and collective grievances.

Therefore, our discussion will take as both given and *desirable* the Enlightenment values of rational inquiry, socioreligious tolerance, and inalienable rights. Such values will form the framework for the argument that follows.

Now seems a good moment to lay our cards on the table. What follows is not going to be a neutral examination of CRT, Me Too, and transgenderism. As you've likely gathered, I am of the correspondence-with-reality tribe, which puts me in the opposition camp when it comes to CRT, Me Too, and transgenderism. But that doesn't mean that every issue we're about to analyze is cut and dried. Power, for example, may not *determine* what's true, but power has a lot to do with whose voices get heard, which opinions are taken seriously, whose ox is gored and how often. You're reading this book, which argues that truth is a correspondence with reality rather than a function of power, because a powerful entity—an established publishing house—has brought it to market. I became known to that publishing house because other powerful entities—state universities, national periodicals, and intellectual journals—have provided me with platforms to set my opinions before the public. It would be facetious, and false, of me to claim that power plays no role in the discovery and dissemination of truth. It does. Those on the other side of the cultural schism are not wrong to point that out.

Nor are they wrong to highlight the subjective element in our experience of reality. That element exists. It's real. Each of us perceives the world subjectively, which means that perception is never without bias. Even though reality is "out there," as it always has been—getting up in your face, not giving a damn about your feelings, forcing you to make adjustments, never quite cooperating with your best laid plans—you don't have unfiltered access to it. There is indeed a filter; that filter is *you*. Because of who you are, because of your history, habits, and prejudices, because of your natural, inescapable you-ness, you've got your own quirky way of perceiving reality…and I've got mine. And though there's lots of overlap, no two people perceive reality in precisely the same way. Much of the time, our differences in perception are trivial: *Is this shirt royal blue or navy?* Occasionally, though, our differences in perception carry huge consequences: *Did our date last night end in consensual sex or in a sexual assault?*

The fact that no one gets reality unfiltered, however, doesn't mean that everyone's perception of it is equally valid. So, for example, if you say that police violence is the primary threat to the lives of young black men, you are objectively wrong. You are saying an untrue thing. You are propagating misinformation. You are spreading fake news.

Even if you feel it in your bones. Even if you are a member of a historically marginalized group. Even if you yourself are a young black man, and you are speaking from "lived experience," you've still got to make the case for the truth of your statement; and in this instance, as we'll discuss below, the case cannot be made. Because *in reality* police violence is not the primary threat to the lives of young black men. Evidence and logic point unequivocally at other threats—primarily, other young black men. Evidence and logic are the things that enable us to work through our filters, even though the filters never come off.

The more attentive we are to evidence and logic, the less our filters distort what we see.

To repeat: there is no democracy of truth. The earth *objectively* revolves around the sun. You don't get to vote on it. You have no more power to alter objective truth than the Catholic Church did when confronted with Galileo's astronomical evidence. If you're powerful enough, as the Church then was, you can make Galileo recant. You can make him cry "aunt-with-balls." But you cannot affect what's objectively true.

Objective truth is revealed by a careful examination of evidence and the application of logic to that evidence. Objective truth is true regardless of our subjective feelings about it because it is anchored in the *object* of the belief or proposition; it is a relationship between out-there and in-here, an alignment between the two. Objective truth forces itself on us. Objective truth is oppressive, at times tyrannical. It's not merely undemocratic; it's *anti*-democratic.

The only way to establish a democracy of truth would be to reject the idea of objective truth, to reject the possibility that human beings are capable of thinking or saying objectively true things, things that correspond with reality. Which is nonsense. The logic doesn't work. You can't claim that objective truth cannot be had without also claiming that your claim is objectively true. If you're right, therefore, you're wrong. And if you're wrong, you're still wrong.

The fact that a growing number of highly credentialed people are making that claim, logic be damned, is at the heart of America's current intellectual crisis. Not because their claim is tenable—it isn't, not even slightly—but because their position is in a sense logically invincible. How effective is a logical critique of a position that literally defies logic? Don't get me wrong. Logical critiques are necessary exercises, and the pages that follow are full of them. But given the nature of this particular crisis, logical critiques may ultimately be toothless.

So what remains? Let me suggest one possibility: ridicule. Ridiculous arguments deserve ridicule, and many of the arguments put forward by advocates for Critical Race Theory, the Me Too movement, and transgender-recognition are indeed ridiculous. Therefore, in addition to logical critiques, you will find regular doses of ridicule in the pages that follow. It's a method of last resort, but I think it's warranted.

It's the right tool for the job.

CHAPTER ONE

A Brief History of Subjectivism

Advocates for Critical Race Theory, the Me Too movement, and transgender-recognition are often grouped under the umbrella term "Woke." There are sound political reasons for the grouping; if you turn up at their rallies, you'll notice lots of overlap in faces, signage, and rhythmic chants. These, however, speak less to their specific agendas and more to the happenstance of a shared dislike of NASCAR, Wall Street, and straight white guys who drink cheap beer and wear their baseball caps backward.

That shared dislike is neither entirely coincidental nor entirely symbolic. Class consciousness (in both directions) is at work, as are socioeconomic interests. But CRT, Me Too, and transgenderism are also related on a more fundamental level. Underpinning them all is a line of subjectivist error that is neither especially new nor very hard to grasp. What *is* new is the intellectual climate that has enabled devotees of that error to join forces and ascend to positions of dominance in various cultural institutions. That ascent would be unimaginable if the institutions housed a critical mass of philosophically literate minds. They don't, as will become evident below.

To understand how CRT, Me Too, and transgenderism are three especially noxious runoffs of a centuries-old, nonsense-polluted stream, we must delve briefly into the history of subjectivism.

Subjectivism, in philosophy, is an exaggerated, relativistic form of idealism. The term *idealism*, however, is ambiguous. Its popular meanings—a devotion to high-minded goals, or a belief that good will triumph over evil—have little to do with its philosophical sense. But even in philosophy, the usage can be tricky. Plato is often erroneously identified as an idealist because he argues that a realm of universal ideas, or forms, is realer than the world experienced through our senses. Likewise, René Descartes is often misclassified because he begins his philosophical project by looking inward rather than outward for a bedrock certitude. On the other hand, Plato and Descartes are both instrumental in the development of idealism as a philosophical approach. Further complicating matters is the fact that even among bona fide idealists such as Berkeley, Kant, and Hegel, their disagreements are so basic that they almost outweigh their commonalities.

Still, to get at subjectivism, we have to begin with idealism, which is the belief that mental objects, ethereal though they may seem, are more basic, or take priority over, or perhaps even constitute what is usually described as reality. It's not a matter of our experience of reality being filtered through our perceptions and ideas; it's a matter of our perceptions and ideas being what we experience.

The most straightforward way to make sense of idealism is in contrast with *realism*—which, as the name suggests, is the belief that reality is substantial, that it exists independently of our perceptions and ideas, that we have access to it, and that the pursuit of truth is an effort to organize our perceptions and ideas in ways that correspond with it. Realism is the common sense view of the world I referenced in the introduction. The fact that realism is commonsensical is, for many philosophers, a strike against it.

Here is a less abstract way to think about the idealism-realism divide: Imagine Steph Curry dribbling a basketball. Now focus on the basketball. It's round. It's grainy. It's bouncy. Those are properties it shares with all basketballs, substantial properties, essential to the thing's "basketball-ness." Curry's basketball has other attributes as well. It's dark brown. It's got the word "Wilson" stamped on it. It's being dribbled by Steph Curry. Those attributes are nonessential. You could easily have a red, white, and blue basketball instead of a dark brown one. Or a basketball with a "Spalding" stamp. Or a basketball being dribbled by LeBron James.

Roundness, graininess, and bounciness are essential to every basketball. You cannot have a basketball without those properties. They are, as I said, *substantial* properties; they are elements of the basketball's substance. Color, brand, and current dribbler are nonessential; they are *accidental* attributes. Individual things are made up of a substance and accidents. The substance is how you determine what a thing is. Accidents are how you distinguish one thing from another of the same kind. The brown Wilson basketball Steph Curry is dribbling is an individual thing, made up of a substance (its basketball-ness) and accidents (its color, brand, and dribbler). It is one instance of a basketball.

Notice that you can take away the basketball's accidental attributes and still have a basketball. But you can't take away any of its substantial properties. If you do that, you no longer have a basketball. If you want to know what a thing is, you're inquiring about its substance. If you want to know which specific thing you're referring to, you're inquiring about its accidents. That's how you acquire knowledge. But knowledge is always finite. You'll never know *everything* about the basketball; you'll never know everything about anything. Even if you've got a good grip on the specific basketball Steph Curry is dribbling, you likely don't know where, when, or by what exact process it was made. Even if you knew all of that, you still would not know the names of the people who packaged and shipped it, or the names of everyone who has ever handled it, or the quantum state of its subatomic particles. Here is what you do know, however, if you are a realist: it exists independently of your perceptions of it. The basketball doesn't cease to be when you turn out the lights in the gym. Which means, at minimum, even if you don't know what a basketball is used for, and even if you don't know who Steph Curry is, or why he's bouncing that round, brown, grainy thing up and down, you do grasp the reality of the basketball.

That's realism. To which the idealist replies, "Not so fast."

Idealism foregrounds not reality but perception. What do you really and truly know about Steph Curry's basketball? Only what your senses register, what you can see, hear, smell, touch, and taste. So you know its roundness, brownness, bounciness, graininess, "Wilson" stamp, and so forth. You know the *thwap* sound it makes each time it hits the floor of the gym. If you cared to lick it, you'd know what it tastes like. What else? The idealist answers nothing. You know the sum of what you perceive with your senses…and nothing else. That spiel I just went into about substance and accidents? To an idealist, that's nothing more than an attempt to sort sense perceptions into a rational order. Rational order makes us feel good; it makes us feel as though we're acquiring knowledge of the world. But why is a substantial property more important than an accidental attribute? Your senses take in information. They don't create hierarchies: this attribute is crucial; this one isn't. What we're getting from our senses is just a stream of perceptions. The order we impose on those perceptions comes from us; the order isn't found in the object itself. All we're doing, in the final analysis, is rearranging perceptions into ideas. The entire process is internal; it is going on between our ears. It is unconnected to the object, the actual basketball. We have no direct experience of "basketball-ness." What we've got is a steady flow of perceptions that, for the sake of convenience, we mentally rope to the word "basketball." That flow of perceptions is what we know, not the underlying thing…if there is an underlying thing.

Reality, according to the idealist, *may* be out there, a ginormous universe of stuff independent of our perceptions of it. But even if that universe *is* out there, we have no way to get at it except through our perceptions—which are the only things we know *directly*. You and I are inward beings, creatures of consciousness. Whatever, if anything, is outside, has to pass through our sense organs in order for us to become aware of it. So our awareness of it is never direct; it is always mediated by our perceptions. We know our perceptions of things, not things-in-themselves. Maybe there is an actual basketball-substance that accounts for those perceptions we associate with it, and maybe there isn't. Idealists bicker over that point. But what they agree on is that even if there is an actual basketball-substance, one that exists independently of our perceiving it, we have no direct access to it. We fool ourselves to think we know a thing or two about reality; we know a thing or two about our perceptions of the reality.

Do idealists honestly believe what they claim to believe? Do they honestly think that a tree (to switch to a more famous example) has no substantial properties, that it is merely a collection of accidental attributes that exist only if perceived, and thus that if a tree falls in the forest and no one hears it, it makes no sound? That's hard to say. What I *can* say is that I have never met anyone who *acted* as though reality did not exist apart from our perceptions, who blithely strolled into oncoming traffic confident that his perceptions, the mere phenomena of his own consciousness, could do him no bodily harm. When asked his opinion of philosophical idealism, eighteenth-century British poet, playwright, literary critic, and inveterate wiseass Samuel Johnson famously kicked a stone and said, "I refute it *thus*."

If the reality of reality is obvious, if indeed it is self-evident, how did a philosophical movement such as idealism ever get off the ground? Its origins can be traced back at least to Plato (c. 427–347 BC)—though, to repeat, while he wrote a great deal about "ideas," Plato himself was decidedly *not* an idealist. Yet in his dialogue *The Republic*, he provides a vastly influential account of the world of our ordinary experience, suggesting that what seems to be reality may not be real. According to Plato, human beings live in a metaphoric cave. We're chained in place, only able to face the back wall, observing shadows cast against it by objects behind us. To cast shadows, however, you need light. That light is coming from a fire near the entrance of the cave. The light from the fire is hitting those objects behind us—the ones we cannot see because of our chains—and producing the shadows on the wall. Because the shadows are all we see, we mistake them for reality. But *in reality* the shadows are insubstantial; they are a distraction. To get at what's truly real, we must break our chains, turn around, and find our way out of the cave. Only outside the cave, in a realm of pure and eternal ideas (or "forms"), are we able to experience reality.

What does Plato mean when he talks about pure and eternal ideas? Let's return to Steph Curry's basketball. For Plato, basketball-ness is realer than any individual basketball. Individual basketballs change; they get worn down, warped, and punctured; they come into and go out of existence. But basketball-ness never changes. It is a pure and eternal idea, a perfect form from which Steph Curry's basketball, LeBron James's basketball, and even that beat up old basketball rolling around the floor of your garage derive their essences. It seems to us that each basketball we pick up and dribble is real. But Plato is arguing that those sense-detectable basketballs are like the shadows on the back wall of the cave. It is the pure and eternal idea of basketball-ness, found only outside of the cave, that is real.

Plato's suggestion that we must break our chains in order to discover what's real underscores the fact that he thinks reality exists independently of our perceptions. If he were an idealist, or even a proto-idealist, the shadows on the back wall of the cave would be no more or less real than the objects casting them, or the fire behind the objects, or the world outside the cave. On the contrary, Plato insists that the struggle to escape the cave, to see past transitory appearances, to *reason beyond* transitory appearances, and to grasp what's real and unchanging, makes life worth living. He points us outward rather than inward, with an eye toward correspondence rather than self-projection.

Nevertheless, the notion that the shadowy, occasionally baffling, constantly changing world of our ordinary experience *isn't* real had a profound and lasting influence on later philosophers. One of them was Descartes (1596–1650). Descartes isn't exactly an idealist either, though like Plato he is an idealist-inspirer. Starting from a position of universal doubt—taking nothing whatsoever (or so he imagined) for granted—Descartes sets out to discover whether he can know anything *with absolute certainty*. He finds that he can doubt everything he's been taught since he has no way to be absolutely certain about the reliability of the people who taught him. He can also doubt the information he receives through his senses since his senses often mislead him; that sound of a gunshot in the distance may turn out to be a firecracker. And if he can doubt sense information, he can doubt the existence of his own body since not only is his body the entryway for sense data, his body is itself revealed to him through his senses. How can he be *certain* that an evil demon isn't fooling him into imagining that he has arms and legs? Human beings, Descartes notes, are notoriously fallible in judging what's real. What seems real as he sleeps proves to be unreal the moment he awakes…which means that, for all he knows, he may be dreaming at that very moment. His waking experience of the world may itself be a dream.

Finally, Descartes concludes that the one thing he cannot doubt is the fact that he is doubting. He cannot think that he is not thinking. He is a thinking being, a rational soul capable of rational thought. Even if all else is suspect, he cannot entertain the thought that he isn't engaged in thought. *Cogito, ergo sum.* I think, therefore I am. That's his baseline, his absolute certainty. He exists. Now all he's got to do is figure out if the material world also exists.

It's an ironic twist. Prior to Descartes, philosophers tended to take the world of our immediate experience as a given and, from that commonsensical starting point, attempt to figure out whether the soul exists. Descartes reverses that. He takes the soul as given and attempts to figure out if the world of our immediate experience exists. How do you get from in-here certainty to out-there certainty? Descartes is able to do so, to his own satisfaction, by way of God. He has a concept of God, a perfect Being, in his mind, and it cannot have come from anywhere except from God himself—because there is no perfect being in Descartes's immediate experience from which to derive such a concept. To be perfect, furthermore, is necessarily to exist, since existence is greater than nonexistence; a perfect being by definition *must* exist, or else it wouldn't be perfect. God therefore exists. (For the record, Descartes here is reiterating the ontological argument for God's existence, developed in its most famous form by the medieval theologian Saint Anselm.) More to the point, for Descartes's purpose, a perfect being would not engage in intentional deception of imperfect beings. It is not in God's nature to trick us into thinking the material world exists. "But once I perceived that there is a God, and also understood at the same time that everything else depends on him, and that he is not a deceiver, I then concluded that everything I clearly and distinctly perceive is necessarily true."[5]

Therefore, the material world must also exist.

That's how Descartes got from in-here to out-there. He stepped over the God-bridge: "And thus I see plainly that the certainty and truth of every science depends exclusively on the knowledge of the true God, to the extent that, prior to becoming aware of him, I was incapable of achieving perfect knowledge about anything else."[6] Certainty about his own existence led him to certainty about God's existence; certainty about God's existence led him to certainty about the existence of the material world and to the potential correspondence of his thoughts to reality. That, in turn, made knowledge possible; if you study the world carefully, you will discover truth and acquire knowledge. Religious faith took Descartes where he needed to go. It actuated his entire intellectual program. He could not get there on the basis of reason alone; for Descartes, there was no bridge from the internal *cogito* to the external world without God. That's the reason subsequent thinkers, including Locke, Hume, and Kant, who did not want their systematic natural philosophies to rest on supernatural faith, severely criticized Descartes's logic. Without intending to do so, however, Descartes ushered mind-body duality to the forefront of philosophical inquiry—and inspired more radical versions of idealism.

That radicalism was given voice, most notably, by the British clergyman and philosopher George Berkeley (1685–1753). "The table I write on, I say, exists," he argues, "that is, I see and feel it; and if I were out of my study, I should say it existed, meaning thereby that if I was in my study, I might perceive it, or that some other spirit actually does perceive it."[7] If, however, no one were around to perceive his desk, it would cease to exist. Berkeley's claim, as counterintuitive as claims come, turns on the meaning of "to exist." In order to exist, a thing must be perceived; it must register as a cluster of perceptions. There is no underlying substance, nothing apart from our experience of it. "What are the forementioned objects but the things we perceive by sense, and what do we perceive besides our own ideas or sensations; and is it not plainly repugnant that any of these or any combination of them should exist unperceived?"[8] To be is to be perceived. *Esse est percipi.* That's the position he is taking.

Let's go back to that tree to illustrate his point. When you encounter a tree, you perceive a range of details: the way it juts out of the ground, the thickness and rotundity of its trunk, the angling and forking of its branches, the tone and texture of its bark, the color and shape of its leaves, the rustle of its leaves in the wind, perhaps even the earthy, vaguely musty scent it emits. These sense perceptions register in your mind. But what is the underlying reality, the substance? For Berkeley, there is none. Your perceptions are the totality of that tree...for you.

What if your perceptions are wrong?

But how can they be wrong? Your perceptions, after all, are *your* perceptions. Whatever your perceptions are, that's what the tree is. The same holds true for me. When I come along, my perceptions of the tree are what the tree is. What if your perceptions and mine don't match? Is one of us right and one of us wrong? No, because there is no underlying substance; there is no *independently existing* tree against which to compare and evaluate our perceptions.

Does that mean that the tree pops in and out of being? Not exactly. Berkeley, in a very bishop-like move, speculates that the tree's existence *does* persist—except not in a mind-independent reality, but in the mind of God. (You can hear the echo of Descartes clearly at this point.) Because God's mind has no off switch, and because he is omnipresent, he perpetually perceives the tree. Even if you and I aren't around to perceive it with our finite organs of perception and limited span of attention, God is always everywhere in his infinitude...and thus, in a sense, holds the tree in existence through his divine perception. But as far as you and I are concerned, the tree may as well not exist when we're not in the vicinity.

Existence, according to Berkeley, is conferred by the *subject* doing the perceiving; it is not a property of an *object* being perceived. Existence is subjective rather than objective. If you follow his logic, however, you run headlong into at least two major difficulties. The first is the reality of other people. If I, a perceiving subject, exist independently of the perceptions of other people, do other people likewise exist independently of mine? Or do other people exist only in the mind of God in order for me to perceive them from time to time? The former idea seems inconsistent with Berkeley's central thesis. The latter seems solipsistic.

Even worse for Berkeley, if existence is conferred by perceptions, if indeed "to be is to be perceived," then what causes our perceptions? Where do they come from? How do they get to our senses?

Such objections led the German philosopher Immanuel Kant (1724–1804) to reject Berkeley's version of idealism. Kant argues that although we only have direct experience of the phenomena of our consciousness, those phenomena must originate from independently existing things. The law of causality is integral to the working of our consciousness, where those phenomena live. No causality, no consciousness. There is no other way for us to think except in terms of causes and effects. It is thus literally inconceivable that our perceptions come to us uncaused. They must be caused by, and therefore rooted in, an objective reality. Things-in-themselves are objectively real, according to Kant, but he doesn't think we can get at them. We can *infer* their existence, since they cause our perceptions, but we are ultimately cut off from things-in-themselves by those very perceptions—which, again, are the only things we experience directly.

Kant therefore also rejects the suggestion that our knowledge is limited to what we perceive. The very fact that we know, that we really and truly *know*, that every effect has a cause proves that we know more than our perceptions. The law of causality is known to us as certainly as anything is known to us, although it's not something we perceive in the same way that we perceive a basketball or a tree. It's a different kind of knowledge. We also know ideas that are true by definition—every triangle has three sides, for example—even if triangles are not, strictly speaking, things-in-themselves, even if they don't exist in the real, three-dimensional world.

Though he accepts the existence of things-in-themselves, Kant is no realist. Rather, he has a more complex, systematized version of idealism in mind. But when push comes to shove, Kant, like Berkeley, believes that our perceptions, not things-in-themselves, are the only things we experience *directly*. "…everything intuited in space and time, all objects of a possible experience, are nothing but phenomena, that is, mere representations; and that these, as presented to us…have no self-subsistent existence apart from human thought."[9] To be sure, things-in-themselves are out there beyond our ken. Their being doesn't depend on our perception of them. They don't go away whenever we blink.

Kant's idealism, thus, is not as radical as Berkeley's since Kant accepts the existence of objective reality, opaque to us though it is, and invents a detailed system to classify other types of knowledge—what is definitionally true goes in one box, for example, and what seems likely true goes in another. But he's still arguing that the nature of objective reality, of things-in-themselves, is unknowable. That makes Kant, despite his many ingenious categorizations, an idealist.

From a realist perspective, Kant's views are less egregiously wrong than Berkeley's. But both have fallen victim to the same fundamental error, which is the belief that because your experience of reality is *mediated by* your perceptions, your experience is *of* your perceptions. They are confusing the means of perceiving for the thing being perceived. It's not as convoluted as it sounds. Suppose a naked woman is strolling through Times Square. If I stare at her, as I am likely to do, my eye will register her image. Literally, an image of her will appear on the fluid surface of my eye. Her image will also appear on the surface of the eye of the guy standing next to me, who happens to be my friend Sal. But suppose Sal has glaucoma. Her image will therefore appear clouded on the surface of his eye.

My image of the naked woman is clearly defined. Sal's is cloudy. Does that mean we're looking at two different naked women? The realist answers *of course not.* Because Sal and I are not looking at the images on the surfaces of our eyes. We're looking *through* those images *at* an actual naked woman. The surface images on our eyes are merely instruments by which we take in the *hubba hubba* of her. If I point a telescope at the moon—you're still thinking about the naked woman, aren't you?—I'm not studying teensy weensy pictures that register on the surface of the lens of the telescope; I'm studying the moon itself, the rock and metal substance, the cratered soil Neil Armstrong walked on, the big round object revolving around the earth, generating gravity, drawing the terrestrial tides in and out.

Here is what the realist understands: knowledge begins with sense perception. But it doesn't end there. Through sense perception, we are able to establish that an object exists and to differentiate it from other objects; we are also able to acquire bits of basic information about the object such as its appearance, sound, smell, taste, and texture. That's when our intellect takes over. Our intellect sifts through the information supplied by our senses and begins to apprehend the essential and nonessential qualities of the object. It makes connections and draws distinctions by which to categorize the object, by which to determine its substantial constituents, its logical origin and natural end, and its relation to other objects. Thus, we rise from *perception* to *conception*. That is the main function of the intellect, to generate concepts. But the intellect has another trick up its metaphoric sleeve, a critical one. It can also train its sights on our organs of sense perception. It can take into account any defects it discovers—such as my friend Sal's glaucoma—and correct for those defects to arrive at an accurate interpretation of the image he perceives. The cloudiness is not an attribute of the naked woman. The cloudiness is an attribute of Sal's eyes.

To summarize: The realist says that we can know the world beyond our perceptions, and that truth consists of thinking and saying things that correspond with the state of that world. The idealist says that our perceptions are the only things we truly know, and therefore that truth cannot be a correspondence. That's the traditional debate between realism and idealism.

Subjectivism enters the fray as an expansion, celebration, and practical application of the radical form of idealism put forward by Berkeley. Certainly, it was not his intention to lay a philosophical groundwork for a leveling of beliefs. But he did so anyway. If there is no objective world independent of our perceptions, then there can be no reality check for our beliefs. Hence, all of our beliefs are ultimately groundless. Which means they're equal. Which means no one can ever tell you you've got your facts wrong. Your perceptions are as true as anyone else's; your lived experience is as valid and authoritative as anyone else's. If you're passionate enough about what you *believe*, it becomes what you *know*. Belief and knowledge converge. Who's to say otherwise? Other people, who may or may not exist? What are they going to say? That your beliefs don't correspond with the state of things-in-themselves, to which we have no direct access?

You know what you know.

The world is your oyster. If you perceive it to be an oyster… in which case it is, and it's yours.

It is at this point in contemporary discussions of philosophy that you will often hear professors in the humanities and social sciences defend subjectivism by invoking Einstein's Theory of Relativity or Heisenberg's Uncertainty Principle in order to claim that "everything is relative" or that "nothing is certain"—and, thus, that the notion of truth as a correspondence between belief and reality is hopelessly naïve.

The first thing to note is that you don't hear such claims put forward by trained physicists. That's because trained physicists actually understand what Einstein and Heisenberg were saying, and both of them were saying, explicitly, that their theories corresponded with reality—in other words, that their theories were objectively true. Einstein began with the premise that the speed of light is always the same (so there goes your "everything is relative" idea) and, from that premise, deduced that measurement of objects in motion, especially at high velocities, could not be as straightforward as had been previously thought—that the position of the observer, with respect to the object in motion, has to be taken into account, that measurement is *relative* to position. The details of the theory are beyond our purposes here. Notice, however, that Einstein isn't arguing for the plurality of truth. Rather, he is saying that from any specific position, there will still be one and only one true measurement of the motion of an object, and that that one true measurement is calculable and in no sense open to negotiation.

Likewise, Heisenberg's Uncertainty Principle asserts an objective truth in the form of a complex mathematical equation: the range of variables of a particle's possible locations multiplied by the range of variables of the particle's possible momentums is greater-than-or-equal-to Planck's constant divided by 4π.

As before, the details are not crucial for our purposes. The upshot is that as our capacity to measure where a particle is found increases, our capacity to measure where the particle is going decreases—because when you multiply the two numbers together, the result must always be greater-than-or-equal-to a definite number. That definite number, once again, is Planck's constant divided by 4π.

So you've got three numbers in a relationship: A x B = C. (Let's treat *greater-than-or-equal-to* as plain old *equals* for the sake of making things clearer.) Since C never changes—it's always Planck's constant divided by 4π—if you make A bigger, B has to get smaller, and if you make B bigger, A has to get smaller. Far from showing that "nothing is certain," Heisenberg's theory asserts that we know *precisely* the relationship between the range of variability in a particle's location and momentum, and the fact that the two variables are inversely proportional to one another means that our capacity to measure one affects our capacity to measure the other.

Thus, the next time a humanities or social science professor steps to a podium and begins to blather about how uncertainty is a feature of the universe, and thus subjectivism is the way of all sophisticates, you may want to ask him if that means Planck's constant isn't constant.

The truth of the matter—and this general principle is useful to bear in mind for the specific discussions that follow—is that humanities and social science professors who cite the theories of Einstein or Heisenberg to argue that objective truth cannot be had are bluffing. They don't know what they're talking about, and they're relying on their audience not knowing what they're talking about either. The bluff works because their audience consists primarily of other humanities and social science professors—who know enough to revere the two names, Einstein and Heisenberg, but not enough to understand, in even a cursory way, the theories themselves.

The fact that it works, that humanities and social science professors regularly bluff one another, should not come as a shock. There is no arena on earth, except perhaps the World Series of Poker, more rife with bluff than academia, and there is no more entrenched and influential bluff in academia than *postmodernism*, which is the final *–ism* we must consider before getting to the excesses, absurdities, and perversities of the present intellectual moment.

Postmodernism is a term that has been crowbarred into contemporary parlance notwithstanding the fact that it defies straightforward definition. Perhaps the easiest way to grasp postmodernism is not as a theory but rather as an attitude. It's a kind of ironic disdain for the entire project of the Enlightenment, including the core belief that reason is a tool of human flourishing, that the axioms of logic are universal, and that the subordination of passion and appetite to rational analysis ennobles the species. Postmodernism shares with subjectivism the denial that we have access to a reality that exists independently of our perceptions. It shares with Marxism a denial that human nature is fixed; human nature, according to postmodernists, is shaped by socioeconomic and cultural forces.

But wait! How can postmodernists defend their belief about the malleability of human nature except by arguing that malleability is a substantial property of human nature, that human nature is *in reality* like that? Isn't that an obvious logical contradiction?

Here we come to the great postmodern trump card: Why is a logical contradiction a problem? Logic is a social construct; there are no universal logical laws. Postmodernism, therefore, affords a profoundly silly but especially potent defense of

Berkeley's radical idealism against Kant's critique: *Who says that our perceptions require causes?* The law of causality, which Kant takes as axiomatic, is nothing more than a mental habit passed off by straight white European males as the one and only operating system of reality. So, too, the law of noncontradiction is binding within a Eurocentric framework of binary thinking; but what about nonbinary frameworks? The hierarchy that sets binary frameworks above nonbinary frameworks is itself a construct; it is nothing more than an expression of European males' will-to-power.

The law of noncontradiction definitely doesn't bind postmodernists. Thus, Jacques Derrida (1930–2004), international man of double-talk, states that one of his foundational concepts, the *arche-trace*, is "contradictory and not acceptable within the logic of identity."[10] Thereafter, he coughs up an argument-shaped hairball of sentences, taking the arche-trace as his starting point, before concluding, "The trace is in fact the absolute origin of sense in general. Which amounts to saying once again that there is no absolute origin of sense in general."[11]

Nor is his arche-trace gag a one-off. *Au contraire*! In his book *Dissémination*, Derrida writes: "It is thus not simply false to say that Mallarmé is a Platonist or a Hegelian. But it is above all not true.... And vice versa."[12]

Why is Derrida's flouting of the law of noncontradiction a big deal? Because the outcome is cognitive silence; you cannot write or speak or even *think* a logically meaningful sentence without taking the law of noncontradiction for granted. So, for example, if I state "John Lennon *was* a member of the Beatles," I'm also denying the contradictory statement, "John Lennon *was not* a member of the Beatles"—or else I'm not saying anything about John Lennon. The first statement *must* rule out the second. Remember how Descartes's realization that he *was* thinking ruled out the possibility that he *was not* thinking? That's the law of noncontradiction, which means that the law of noncontradiction precedes even "I think, therefore I am." This is such a basic point that to explain it seems to belabor the obvious.

But let's up the emotional stakes. If I put forward a truly heinous proposition such as "Adolf Hitler was a man who promoted the well-being of all people," your natural response will be to cite the genocidal persecutions of Jews, Slavs, and homosexuals under the Nazi regime he led. You cite these instances in order to establish the denial, or contradictory, of my heinous proposition, in other words, "Hitler was not a man who promoted the well-being of all people." Why do you seek to establish the contradictory? Because you know, intuitively, that the two propositions, the assertion and denial, cannot be held at the same time; thus, the moment you can convince me that Hitler *was not* a man who promoted the well-being of all people, I am forced to abandon the proposition that Hitler *was* a man who promoted the well-being of all people.

Contradictory propositions do not merely go against one another. They *unsay* one another. They cancel one another out. The only logical way to read a writer who rejects the law of noncontradiction, who freely and openly contradicts himself, is mentally to insert the words, "or not" after each of his sentences.

That's the only way to read Derrida. That's the only way to read many of the leading lights of postmodernism. For example, the renowned literary critic Roland Barthes (1915–1980) describes his ideal reader as one,

> who abolishes within himself all barriers, all classes, all exclusions...by simple discard of that old specter: logical contradiction; who mixes every language, even those said to be incompatible; who silently accepts every charge of illogicality, of incongruity; who remains passive in the face of Socratic irony (leading the interlocutor to the supreme disgrace: self-contradiction) and legal terrorism (how much penal evidence is based on a psychology of consistency!).[13]

Thus, the rapist who has been convicted on the grounds that he contradicted himself in his own defense, insisting that he both was and was not at the scene of the attack, is the victim of "legal terrorism."

The third of postmodernism's triumvirate of stooges, Michel Foucault (1926–1984), focuses his indignation on common sense because it carries, "the tyranny of goodwill, the obligation to think 'in common' with others, the domination of a pedagogical model, and most importantly—the exclusion of stupidity."[14] The demands of common sense inspire in us a reflexive desire to avoid stupidity, Foucault says; for that reason, "we must liberate ourselves from these constraints; and in perverting this morality, philosophy itself is disoriented."

But how can we put stupidity into practice? According to Foucault, stupidity,

> requires thought without contradiction, without dialectics, without negation; thought that accepts divergence; affirmative thought whose

> instrument is disjunction.... What is the answer to the question? The problem. How is the problem resolved? By displacing the question.[15]

Note especially Foucault's last two lines. It seems bizarre to think that stupidity would have a methodology of its own, yet it does. It is called "deconstruction." It is a mode of pseudo-analysis, a sequence of rhetorical feints and demurrals, a kind of verbal sleight of hand. First, you tease out secondary and tertiary senses of individual lines, words, or even syllables in order to show how a text contradicts what it seems clearly to be saying; next, you free-associate your way to a few philosophical banalities or outright non sequiturs; finally, you top off the mishmash with a glaze of intentionally impenetrable jargon so that if a sad sack reader is foolish enough to attempt to make sense of what you're talking about, he'll get bogged down in the sticky stuff before he can figure out you're not talking about anything in particular.

Here's how it works, minus the jargon: Suppose I say that my first name is Mark. The postmodernist would deconstruct that claim. He might point out that, on the day I was born, before I was ever "Mark," I was "Baby Goldblatt"—therefore, the claim that my *first* name is Mark is, in a temporal sense at least, false. He might also note that, in terms of social priority, "Goldblatt" is the name by which I'm primarily known at the payroll department at my university; it is also the name by which students primarily address me. What's primary is first. Thus, my first name is *not* Mark. He might then mention that the word "mark," if it is stripped of its nominative sense, connotes a sign by which ownership is claimed—i.e., "to make one's mark." So it is also a territorial signifier, perhaps meant by me to carve out a political space in which I can conduct my relationships on a familiar basis. It is, in short, a deception. Claiming Mark as my "first" name is thus inevitably a political act and an expression of my own will-to-power.

This is deconstruction. It is the methodology of postmodernism. More to the point, *it is the methodology of professional stupidity*. Remarkably, it has persuaded roughly half the humanities and social science professors in the United States—a species whose gullibility ranks them somewhere between nine-year-old boys listening to spooky campfire stories and blissful puppies chasing after nonexistent sticks—into casting aside traditional, empirical ways of gathering and interpreting evidence in favor of vomiting up polysyllabic word salads that are often indistinguishable from parodies of scholarship.[16]

You want *stupid* science? Postmodernist critic Luce Irigaray has you covered: "Is E=mc2 a sexed equation? Perhaps it is. Let us make the hypothesis that it is insofar as it privileges the speed of light over other speeds that are vitally necessary to us. What seems to me to indicate the possibly sexed nature of the equation is not directly its uses by nuclear weapons, rather it is having privileged what goes the fastest."[17]

You want *stupid* metaphysics? Postmodernist critic and translator Gayatri Spivak doesn't disappoint: "…does not thinking seek forever to clamp a dressing over the gaping and violent wound of the impossibility of thought?"[18]

You want the sound of one hand clapping? Postmodernist critic Barbara Johnson declares: "Instead of a simple either/or structure, deconstruction attempts to elaborate a discourse that says neither 'either/or,' nor 'both/and' nor even 'neither/

nor,' while at the same time not totally abandoning these logics either."[19]

You have to be not merely intellectually unserious but indeed hostile to the basic principles of intellectual seriousness to take this nonsense seriously. This is not to suggest that post-modernists don't say interesting things. If you put a sufficient number of words on paper, you'll say interesting things from time to time. But these are aleatory events, rolls of the dice, like a random line of Shakespeare that might emerge from a room full of typing chimpanzees.

How does the corrosive nonsense of postmodernism serve the sociopolitical interests of the Woke? It complements their subjectivism. With its denial that our knowledge extends beyond our perceptions, subjectivism levels the evidentiary playing field; it diminishes the status of empirically gathered data and elevates the status of individual impressions and personal anecdotes over verifiable evidence and reproducible logic.

But a traditional subjectivist is still vulnerable to the charge of irrationality and self-refutation. That's where postmodernism comes into play. It plays with, dances around, and verbally masturbates on whatever empirical evidence *is* presented until what's clear seems obscure, and the motives of critics can be called into question. When all else fails, postmodernism supplies a perpetual get-out-of-losing-arguments-free card: *YOU'RE holding ME to the demands of logic? Seriously? Haven't I, and people like me, suffered enough from the analytical imperialism of Aristotle and his ilk?*

The rhetorical arsenal of the Woke is now complete.

Subjectivism gets them around the charge that their facts are objectively false. How can facts be objectively false if perception defines reality?

Postmodernism gets them around the charge that their reasoning is fallacious. How can reasoning be fallacious when the rules of logic are social constructs?

When you combine the two you get *Woke subjectivism*, an invincible subjectivism, a nihilistic, Nietzschean subjectivism put forward by catchphrase radicals and their excitable acolytes, who, if we take them at their word, imagine themselves as free-thinking idealists and egalitarian liberators. It is a subjectivism in which noise becomes power, and power determines what's true.

CHAPTER TWO

What's So Critical about CRT?

What a Theory Is

According to Kimberlé Crenshaw, one of its earliest and most influential advocates, "Critical race theory [CRT] draws upon several traditions, including poststructuralism, postmodernism, Marxism, feminism, literary criticism, liberalism, and neopragmatism."[20] That means we're going to have to hack through a dense forest of terminological bluff and dorm room agitprop to get at what she's talking about. But before we begin our long, hard slog, let's focus on the clearest and least controversial of the three words: critical race theory.

Simply put, a *theory* is an attempt to explain something, to account for a set of facts that seem otherwise perplexing. Quantum theory is an attempt to explain the paradoxical nature and behavior of subatomic systems. The theory of evolution is an attempt to explain how more complex living organisms, including humans, arose from basic life forms. Theories are not necessarily true. They may or may not correspond with reality, which is a roundabout way of saying they must be falsifiable. Falsified theories—theories that do not correspond with reality, that consistently fail to explain the set of facts they purport to explain—get discarded. If a theory is falsified but not discarded, it isn't really a theory; it's an article of faith. Theories, moreover, are often in competition with one another, at least until one of them clearly seems a better fit for the facts. Among cosmologists, for example, the big bang theory, the idea that the entire universe exploded into existence at a single moment, used to compete with something called the steady state theory, the idea that the universe had always existed and would always exist. That rivalry lasted until observations of cosmic background noise, in the form of radiation, predicted by the big bang theory, consigned the steady state theory to the dustbin of history.

What does Critical Race *Theory* attempt to explain?

The fact that even after the breakthroughs of the Civil Rights Era, even after Supreme Court decisions outlawing discrimination based on ethnicity, even after survey after survey reveals an abiding national consensus in favor of a colorblind society, black Americans, taken as a whole, continue to trail other demographic groups in health outcomes, educational attainment, and a vast array of socioeconomic measures.

What is the theoretical explanation put forward by CRT for the lag?

Racism.

It's a temptingly uncomplicated explanation, and there is a definite plausibility to it. If racism is defined in the traditional way—as the belief, or an action predicated on the belief, that one imprecisely-defined class of ancestrally-connected people is intellectually or morally inferior to another—then American history is surely rife with racism. Foremost, of course, it is rife anti-black racism. Anti-black racism is viewed by many Americans as the nation's original sin: its economic base, dating back to the earliest European settlements, was deepened and broadened by involuntary and uncompensated labor provided by African slaves and their enslaved descendants. It would be difficult to conceive a worse form of exploitation, and it was undeniably rooted in *definitional* racism—the widespread belief among white Europeans, including those who colonized the New World, in the intellectual and moral inferiority of black Africans. For that reason, Americans descended from African slaves, whatever their current situation, have a unique moral claim on the collective conscience of their fellow Americans.

That moral claim, furthermore, extends to *all* other Americans, of every ethnicity, even to those who came here after slavery had been abolished, since later arrivals benefited from that original economic base. Indeed, the claim extends *even to other black Americans who came here of their own volition.* It is, again, a *unique* moral claim. Other minorities have suffered grave injustices and indignities at the hands of various majorities; other demographics have been deprived of rights. None were treated as commodities to be bought and sold; none had generations of their labor stolen. America has become the most powerful engine of prosperity, security, and liberty the world has ever known. The engine mount was built, at least in part, from the broken bones of slaves.

That much is well-nigh indisputable. Nor is it controversial to note that even after the abolition of slavery following the Civil War in 1865, racism continued to serve as a justification for systematic discrimination against black Americans. The codified biases of the Jim Crow era, as well as a vast array of unspoken-but-understood abuses, rooted as before in the widespread perception of black inferiority, may not have totally stymied black advances in health, education, and socioeconomics, but those nods and winks undoubtedly retarded their overall progress.

Finally, even though the civil rights movement of the mid-twentieth century put an end to legalized discrimination, many of those unspoken-but-understood abuses persisted. Here, however, the argument becomes knottier. It is assumed by advocates of CRT that the unspoken-but-understood abuses persist even now, sponsored by ongoing anti-black racism. The nods and winks may be gone. But that's only because the abuses are now embedded in the collective psyche of the nation as well as in the ordinary operation of private and public entities. The knee-capping thus continues. Descendants of slaves are still being robbed of a rightful share of America's prosperity, security, and liberty. The health, educational, and socioeconomic stagnation of black Americans is explained by racism and racism alone.

That is the essence of CRT.

Blurring the Definition of Racism

Notice, however, that to tie off that last loop in the CRT argument, to make the case that racism *remains* a decisive force in health, educational, and sociopolitical outcomes, you need to blur, or at least finagle, the meaning of racism. As you shift from racism as a belief in racial inferiority, or an action predicated on that belief, to racism as a persistent feature of a worldview or a system, you lose the definitional element of consciousness. Beliefs may be widely held, but they're still held by individuals; even if many individuals hold a wrong or insidious belief, unless that belief translates into action, that's a private matter. Nor does a system operate with an awareness of what it is doing. If all of the laws, which are mental constructs, have been made colorblind, and the nodding and winking, which are deliberate acts, are gone, then where does the racism live? To say that racism is an integral feature of a national psychology or a nonconscious system is thus to significantly enlarge the meaning of the term and bring subjectivity into play. There's much less, "Aha!" There's much more, "Mmm hmm!"

It comes as no surprise, therefore, to find the author, activist, and high priest of CRT, Ibram X. Kendi, explicitly redefining racism: "I define it as a collection of racist policies that lead to racial inequity that are substantiated by racist ideas."[21] And again: "Racism is a marriage of racist policies and racist ideas that produces and normalizes racial inequities."[22]

The circularity of such a definition jumps off the page. Using a term to define itself doesn't get you very far toward clarifying its meaning. But let's extend the benefit of the doubt and suppose that Kendi has something clear in mind. Racism, he seems to suggest, is not merely a belief in inferiority, or an action predicated on that belief, but any systemic feature that perpetuates that belief and leads to more discrimination. Whatever makes people *feel* that one group, in this context black people, is intellectually or morally inferior to another, in this context white people, may cause the presumed superior group to behave reflexively in ways that perpetuate the wrongs suffered by the presumed inferior group. In other words, if you continuously observe outcomes that reflect poorly on black people, you will *unconsciously* begin to infer that black people are in some sense "less than"—and adjust your actions in ways (fear, suspicion, avoidance) that deny black people an opportunity to dispel that inference.

Again, it's not an implausible thought.

But enlarging the scope of a term, making it describe more things, comes at a logical cost. You run into *the law of intension and extension.* "Intension" is the internal content of a term, the thought in your mind when you use it, its common definition. "Extension" is what's covered by the term, the range of things to which it applies. The law of intension and extension holds that the further you extend a term, the vaguer it becomes. As you overuse it, the term necessarily means less and less. If I say that all men are artists, I'm draining virtually all of the meaning out of the term "artist." That becomes a problem if I subsequently want to say, "Picasso is an artist." I'm not telling you anything in that case except, "Picasso is a man."

Likewise, Kendi's use of the term "racism" drains it of much of its content. If any outcome that *may* imply an intellectual or moral shortcoming among black people is a de facto instance of racism, then racism has become indistinguishable from the failure of a critical number of black people to meet specific intellectual or moral standards. So, for example, if the video feed from security cameras at the local shopping mall shows a disproportionate number of black people shoplifting, then the video feed is racist. But how can an unedited video feed be racist? What does the word mean at that point?

Take another look at Kendi's definition: "Racism is a marriage of racist policies and racist ideas that produces and normalizes racial inequities." Following that logic, isn't the overrepresentation of black athletes in sports such as football, basketball, and sprinting proof of racism? Doesn't it suggest to many observers that non-black athletes cannot perform at the highest levels? Hasn't that bias become pervasive in society and created stereotypes that hold back non-black athletes? If so, isn't it therefore the work of an anti-racist to reduce the number of black athletes in those sports? Or are we now to imagine that black people are a master race: If they come up short, that's racism at work, yet if they excel, that's not racism but merely the natural order of things?

How can that be? Again, what does racism mean at that point?

You see the analytical difficulties this line of thinking creates. Was American slavery racist? Yes, American slavery was definitionally racist. Was segregation? Yes, again, definitionally. What about white flight? Now it gets slightly harder. You can understand the reasoning of white families who fled the inner cities beginning in the 1960s and 1970s; even if they had no personal animus against black people, and no objection to living next door to black families, and didn't see black people as intellectually or morally inferior, they might have feared, based on statistical evidence, that an influx of black residents would result in more neighborhood crime and poorer school performance, which in turn would drive down their property values. So maybe they were making an economically sound decision to move. But are you bending over backward, in making that argument, to excuse the behavior? Sounds like it to me, though I'd be hesitant to dismiss it out of hand.

But what about draconian prison sentences for users of crack cocaine (who tend to be black) but not users of powder cocaine (who tend to be white)? To reach that judgment, you must first ask how and why the disparity came about. As it happens, the demand for harsher sentencing guidelines for crack users originated with black inner-city residents during the 1970s and 1980s whose neighborhoods were devolving into war zones between rival drug gangs. When this local demand for safe streets bubbled up to the federal level, it was supported by members of the Congressional Black Caucus.[23] The outcome of the draconian guidelines, of course, was to skew black prison populations relative to their overall population numbers; therefore, those guidelines may well have reinforced public perception of black criminality. So the guidelines seem to meet Kendi's systemic definition.

But if the criminal justice system *hadn't* responded to the pleas of black inner-city residents, if it had allowed the violence in their neighborhoods to continue unabated, wouldn't that, by Kendi's definition, also have been a racist strategy? Can both prongs of a fork in the road be racist? Mustn't we ask the same question about, say, stop and frisk policies employed by metropolitan police departments? Those policies have demonstrably had a disparate impact on young black men but also demonstrably saved black lives—since black people continue to be the most frequent victims of inner-city crime. If a policy disproportionately saves black lives but disparately afflicts young black men and contributes to the perception of black criminality, does it still make sense to call that policy racist? More black faces behind bars or more black toes tagged in the morgue: How do you make that call? Even if you decide that the cost-benefit equation for stop and frisk is out of balance, isn't the more reasonable claim that the policy is *misguided* rather than *racist*?

Such questions crop up once you subtract the element of human consciousness from the definition of racism. As soon as you argue that racism can be a feature of nonconscious systems rather than of the human beings who design and inhabit them, you flirt with meaninglessness.

Nowhere is that flirtation more evident than in the charge that standardized testing is inherently racist. "We still think there's something wrong with the kids rather than recognizing their [sic] something wrong with the tests," Kendi wrote in October 2020 in support of an effort to end standardized testing for admission to middle grade "exam schools" in Boston. "Standardized tests have become the most effective racist weapon ever devised to objectively degrade Black and Brown minds and legally exclude their bodies from prestigious schools."[24]

Kendi then lays out his argument:

> Why do Black and Latinx children routinely get lower scores on the standardized tests? Either there's something wrong with the test takers or there's something wrong with the tests. Why are Black and Latinx children routinely under-represented in the exam schools? Either there's something wrong with the Black and Latinx children or there's something wrong with Boston's admissions policies. To say there's something wrong with Black and Latinx

> children is to say racist ideas. And those who say racist ideas, typically deny their ideas are racist.
>
> We need to stop putting down Black and Latinx and Native children. We need to stop putting down low-income White and Asian children. There's something wrong with the test; there's something wrong with the admissions policies—not the kids. We need to radically change our educational system and stop attacking the kids and their caretakers and their teachers.

Well, no. What Kendi is attacking here is not racism but the idea of meritocracy, which he in turn defines as racist because it doesn't yield equal outcomes. That's because it isn't meant to.

The purpose of the standardized test for admission to middle grade "exam schools" in Boston is to gauge the student test-takers' academic progress and potential. If you think that the test is a reliable gauge of such things—and Kendi offers not a shred of evidence to suggest otherwise—then the observation that black and Hispanic kids perform poorly on the test does not necessarily imply "there's something wrong with Black and Latinx [sic] children." It *could* imply that, but it would be one hell of an academic instrument if it were able to pick up on *innate* deficiencies. (More on this notion below.) On the contrary, the observation that black and Hispanic kids perform poorly on a particular test more likely suggests that there's something lacking in their educational preparation that will be difficult to overcome.

It's especially ironic that Kendi would mention low-income Asian children. For even though black and Hispanic kids do indeed score 20 percent lower on the Boston exam than white kids do, Asian kids score seven points *higher*.[25] Indeed, the fact that Asian kids consistently outperform white kids on standardized tests nationwide has in recent decades undercut the traditional argument that the tests are culturally biased—scattered, supposedly, with multiple choice questions about stereotypically white things such as yachting and cucumber sandwiches. If cultural references are indeed decisive in standardized testing, how can it be that Asian students are more attuned than white students to American culture? Nor can the overachievement of Asian students be attributed to economic advantages since they are more likely than white kids to come from low-income households; Asian kids, as a matter of fact, are roughly as likely to come from low-income households as are black or Hispanic kids.[26] Yet for Asian students, standardized tests are an equalizer...whereas for black and Hispanic students they're a millstone.

How is that possible?

One explanation, put forward by San Francisco school board member Alison Collins, is that Asian students, as well as Asian parents and Asian teachers, "use white supremacist thinking to assimilate and 'get ahead.'"[27]

To study hard, according to Collins, to excel on standardized tests, to earn high grades, to exceed expectations, is white supremacist behavior. Asians are therefore complicit in the systemic oppression of black students.

Collins was eventually censured and ousted from her school board position, along with two other CRT advocates, in a city-wide recall vote...which, of course, by the tenets of CRT, shows what happens when you "speak truth to power."[28]

Rinse and repeat.

Kendi's explanation for black underperformance on standardized tests is that the tests themselves are instruments of racism. The tests are *effectively* racist for the very reason that black kids underperform on them, which encourages and engrains a general perception of black inferiority. But—and here is one instance where CRT breaks new intellectual ground—the tests are also *essentially* racist because they demand exactitude.

The Essentialism Trap

CRT, properly understood, is like a three-legged stool. Take away even one of the legs, and the entire enterprise crumbles. The first leg is collective grievance, rooted in undeniable wrongs perpetrated against dark-skinned people by lighter-skinned people. The second is a distinctive type of revisionist historiography in which "lived experience"—the subjective ways people report and interpret their individual and group stories—trumps objectively verifiable and logically analyzed evidence. The third leg is racial essentialism, the belief that different races *properly* have different modes of cognition, different ways of thinking about things, and different ways of knowing what they know. The glue that holds the entire thing together is postmodernism, which (to nullify the metaphor) dissolves standard hierarchical claims that set objectivity over subjectivity and intellect over emotion, thereby acquitting the critical race theorist of the charge of irrationality—because reason itself is seen as another means of oppression.

Now at first glance it may seem odd to suggest that racial essentialism is a necessary component of CRT since CRT advocates often point out, correctly, that racial groupings are social constructs, and that there are no hard and fast, ancestrally-oriented dividing lines in the human species. To be sure, you can divvy up people in various ways, and many visible characteristics (facial features, hair color, height) and invisible characteristics (intellectual and musical aptitudes, susceptibility to disease, perhaps even sexual orientation) are partly or mostly heritable. So it's natural that when certain visible and invisible characteristics cluster—for example, dark skin and athletic potential—to imagine you've hit on a coherent racial category and a common attribute.

You haven't. Racial categories are arbitrary in both definition and number. The 2010 US Census Form, for example, asked respondents to select their race from the following list: White, Black (African American, or Negro), American Indian (or Alaska Native), Asian Indian, Chinese, Filipino, Japanese, Korean, Vietnamese, Other Asian, Native Hawaiian, Guamanian (or Chamorro), Samoan, Other Pacific Islander. Respondents were also invited to check off more than one race…and if none of the listed options struck their fancy, respondents were also welcome to make up their own race. If you're under the impression that racial categories are biologically meaningful divisions, here are the pertinent questions to ask yourself: *Exactly* what are the definitional requisites for membership in any race, *exactly* where are the boundaries, and *exactly* how many races are there?

Perhaps there are answers forthcoming; as yet, no one has produced them.

Why then do CRT advocates simultaneously reject the reality of racial categories yet embrace racial essentialism (a contradiction that would be deadly except in an avowedly postmodern movement)? Because they need to account for the failure of black people to measure up to non-black people in a number of statistically significant ways; they therefore need to argue that the criteria of measurement themselves reflect a bias against black people. To make that case, however, you must presuppose that black people are in some sense *essentially* distinct from non-black people. You must presuppose that, on a fundamental level, black people are wired differently.

Think about it. If black people are wired differently, you have a ready-made narrative of victimization. To take the most obvious example: you have a full explanation for why the scores of black kids lag behind others on standardized tests, and you have compelling proof of how past racism—in this case, the assumption of "white wiring" as the intellectual norm—continues to hold back black people.

The normalization of the way white minds work thus becomes a quintessential tool of white supremacy. That's the premise behind the notorious "Whiteness" education portal sponsored by the Smithsonian's National Museum of African American History and Culture. The original centerpiece of that portal was a chart (later withdrawn, after a public outcry) titled *Aspects and Assumptions of Whiteness and White Culture*. What "aspects" and "assumptions" are we talking about? Here's a partial list:

- Objective, rational, linear thinking
- Cause and effect relationships
- Quantitative emphasis

- Hard work is the key to success
- Work before play
- Heavy value on ownership of goods, space, property
- Plan for the future
- Delayed gratification
- The nuclear family: father, mother, 2.3 children is the ideal social unit
- Follow rigid time schedules
- Decision-making
- Written tradition
- Be polite[29]

These, according to the Smithsonian's National Museum of African American History and Culture, are *essentially* white things. Black people cannot be expected to adapt to them or value them in the same way white people do; it's not in the *nature* of black people to do so.

Of course, the notion that black people are just different didn't spontaneously evolve in the halls of the Smithsonian. It's a commonplace among critical race theorists. So, for example, we hear educational consultant and Columbia University Professor Maria Tope Akinyele explain:

> Black people, we are relational people. We are people of context. Like, it's very Western and European to dissect and analyze and take apart things, whereas [in] Afrocentric schooling or Afrocentric spirituality or African epistemology or ways of knowing, everything is connected. So this is why education is not working for so many students of color because we are

> context-driven people. We can't tell a story without telling the ten things that happened that led up to that moment. There's no such thing as like thinking in isolation—isolating yourself from nature, from your family. It's just not part of our ways of knowing and being in the world. So when we tap into the ways that we understand the world, students are able to make wonderful connections and unleash their brilliance and their wisdom.[30]

Sounds like a straightforward endorsement of racial essentialism. Except twenty minutes later, *in the same YouTube talk*, she recounts a training session she held for a group of predominantly white instructors at which, "....about seventy percent of them did not know that race was a made-up thing. Like *did not know*! And I was like, 'Who is teaching you?' This is disrespect!"

CRT, again, has three legs: Collective grievance. Subjective historiography. And racial essentialism. The glue that holds it together is the postmodernist rejection of rationality as an arbiter of truth. Postmodernism is the reason it's fruitless to point out that Professor Akinyele is contradicting herself. What possible difference would that make to her? What difference *could* it make within a CRT framework?

There's another noteworthy turn of phrase that crops up in her talk, however: *being in the world*. The expectation of, and preference for, logical, linear thinking, Professor Akinyele claims, stymies the progress of black students because it is alien not only to the ways in which they make sense of the world but to their "being in the world." The German philosopher, and occasional Nazi, Martin Heidegger coined the expression in his notoriously indecipherable doorstop of a treatise, *Being and Time*. "Being in the world," for Heidegger, means actively dwelling within, rather than merely inhabiting, the brute fact of your existence. Professor Akinyele's casual reference is thus curious, though it is difficult to determine from the context whether the echo is accidental or intentional.

Let's suppose it's the latter. *Being black in the world*, she seems to be saying, is naturally distinct from *being white in the world*. Race is a substantial quality, something that necessarily goes to the very core of how you exist. It is not constructed, slipped on and off as you pass from one social context to another, but unavoidably lived at every moment you are awake. If you *are* black, there is no other way to live authentically than *as* black, in contradistinction to living as white. It is hard to imagine a more essentialist view of race than the one Professor Akinyele espouses. Nor is her view out of the mainstream among advocates of CRT.

Nowhere is CRT's reliance on racial essentialism more evident than in its theorizing about mathematics. Remember, a theory is an attempt to explain something. The thing to be explained is black underperformance in math.

Black kids, from the earliest grades, trail other demographics in math scores; by the time they reach college, black students are profoundly underrepresented among math majors, and their shortage at the graduate level is startling. Roughly 14 percent of the US population identifies as black. But in 2019, less than 4 percent of PhDs awarded in mathematics and computer sciences (69 out of 1,787) went to black students. The trend also holds for other math-related fields. Only 2 percent of the PhDs awarded in physical and earth sciences (88 out of 3,903) went to black students; 4 percent of the PhDs awarded in engineering (178 out of 4,253) went to black students.

Lest I be accused of ignoring economic realities—such as the cost of a graduate degree—consider that a full 7 percent of total PhDs (2,512 out of 35,274) were awarded to black students. So while black students are underrepresented across the entire range of doctoral fields, their scarcity in STEM subjects is more pronounced. Consider, as well, that doctoral degrees in STEM fields are among the most lucrative of all advanced degrees. It's not the financial burden of graduate study that's chasing black students out of STEM fields. It's something about the fields themselves.

It's the math.

Why do young black people shy away from the subject?

Dr. Deborah Loewenberg Ball, professor of education at the University of Michigan and former Dean of the University of Michigan School of Education, as well as director of its TeachingWorks initiative, thinks she knows the answer. Math, she declares, "is a harbor for whiteness…the very nature of the knowledge and who's produced it, and what has counted as mathematics is itself also dominated by whiteness and by racism."[31]

But how can mathematics, an abstract system of numbers and operations arising out of a set of straightforward axioms, be "dominated" by racism? Even if those axioms weren't true—even if they didn't correspond with reality—they're not secret. They're available to everyone. The playing field therefore seems level. Ah, but it isn't! Because, to return to the Smithsonian's Whiteness and White Culture chart, mathematics normalizes "objective, rational, linear thinking."

What's needed, then, is subjective mathematics!

But the process gets even more insidious, according to Dr. Ball, because "being good at math is seen as being just generally more smart [sic]. And you don't have to go very far to trace that into the racialized history of how we see intelligence and intelligence testing to understand how raced the whole notion of being good at math becomes."[32]

CRT proposes that the working out of equations and application of logic to abstract problems is rife with the normalization of white ways of thinking and knowing (and *being*, according to Professor Akinyele). That normalization in itself would be injurious to black people. But mathematical racism compounds its poisonous effect due to the high esteem in which math is held and the widespread perception that people who are good at math tend to be more intelligent than those who are not.

To rid ourselves of that racism, therefore, we must reconceive the entire enterprise of mathematics and mathematical pedagogy. We must wash out the whiteness, rid math of its perpetual reliance on and reward of objective, rational, linear thinking. Only then will it become friendlier to black students. That's the idea behind Seattle's 2019 Math Ethnic Studies Framework, intended to overhaul instruction in grades K-12. The keynote is struck at the very top of the first page. "Mathematical theory and application," we are informed, "is rooted in the ancient histories of people and empires of color."[33] Somehow, however, those colorful originators of mathematics have gotten cheated out of their legacy. How can their descendants reclaim it?

The Seattle framers have a few ideas:

> Student action, as defined by ethnic studies, is fostering a sense of advocacy, empowerment,

> and action in the students that creates internal motivation to engage in and contribute to their identities as mathematicians. Students will be confident in their ability to construct and decode mathematical knowledge, truth, and beauty so they can contribute to their experiences and the experiences of people in their community.[34]

The priority in math instruction, according to the framework, should not be to assist students in their pursuit of correct answers to math problems but rather to nurture their "sense of advocacy, empowerment and action." Fixation on correct answers is, of course, a white thing; it doesn't allow black students to develop "their identities as mathematicians." What's crucial is that students "construct and decode" (read: *deconstruct*) "mathematical knowledge, truth, and beauty" in order to "contribute to their experiences and the experiences of people in their community." It's the journey, not the destination. The destination is merely a correct answer, a fact. But the *journey* is...wait for it...a story. It's a subjective experience.

Black students don't need to *think* math; they need to *feel* it. They need to feel empowered enough to fight the power. That should be the goal of math instruction. The framework makes this point explicitly: "What does it mean to do math? How important is it to be Right? What is Right? Says Who? What is the difference between being right and being a learner? What does it mean to make a mistake? In the classroom? In my home? In my community?" Not only is the study of math a communal project, it must be seen as part of the struggle against white supremacy: "Who holds power in a mathematical classroom?

Is there a place for power and authority in the math classroom? Who gets to say if an answer is right?"

Indeed, the study of math, if done in the right way, becomes another means to educate yourself in the varieties of systemic racism:

> How is math manipulated to allow inequality and oppression to persist? Who is doing the oppressing? Who does the oppression protect? Who does the oppression harm? Where is there an opportunity to examine systemic oppression? How can math help us understand the impact of economic conditions and systems that contribute to poverty and slave labor?[35]

The ongoing struggle against racist math practices is what animates a 2021 tool kit for math teachers titled, *A Pathway to Equitable Math Instruction: Dismantling Racism in Mathematics Instruction*. The tool kit's authors have loftier goals than teaching kids how to work with numbers: "This tool provides teachers an opportunity to examine their actions, beliefs, and values around teaching mathematics. The framework for deconstructing racism in mathematics offers essential characteristics of antiracist math educators and critical approaches to dismantling white supremacy in math classrooms by making visible the toxic characteristics of white supremacy culture."[36]

So in addition to addition and subtraction, there's going to be deconstruction. But what is to be deconstructed? Primarily, the supposition that "'good' math teaching is about a Eurocentric type of mathematics, devoid of cultural ways of being."[37]

It's another curious phrase: *cultural ways of being.* Is there a culturally specific way of being black? Does that culturally specific way of being black define racial authenticity? If so, does that mean that a black kid who's good at math is being white? Or just pretending to be white?

I could go on[38] (and on[39] and on[40]), but you get the point. Racial essentialism—the idea that black people are just, you know, *different*—is a critical element of Critical Race Theory. They are different from white people, first and foremost, but they are also different, from time to time, from other people of color, especially Asians, whose kids do exceptionally well on standardized math exams and thus become de facto white. Recall here the opinion of Alison Collins, formerly of San Francisco's school board, who suggested that Asian students, parents, and teachers, "use white supremacist thinking to assimilate and 'get ahead.'" (An Asian friend of mine refers to Asians as "Schrodinger's minority"; they're white if you test them, but if you don't test them, they're still people of color.)

If you buy into the idea that black people are innately different, and that their innate differences necessarily result in a culture unique to them—a culture ultimately rooted in a *black epistemology*, a black way of knowing what they know—a lot of CRT's explanatory power follows. Writing for the American Bar Association, Georgetown Law Professor Janel George first asserts (again, correctly) that race is a social construct, yet then explains that CRT entails a "[r]ecognition of the relevance of people's everyday lives to scholarship. This includes embracing the lived experiences of people of color, including those preserved through storytelling, and rejecting deficit-informed research that excludes the epistemologies of people of color."[41]

Because black people have different epistemologies—that is, they have different ways of making sense of things, of knowing what they know—they are *necessarily* more dependent on storytelling. They are *necessarily* less objective in their thinking. They are *necessarily* emotion-driven rather than reason-driven. Expecting black people to conform their thought processes to the way white minds work is like forcing square pegs into round holes. That expectation has them (to mix the metaphor) rowing against the tide from the moment they are born.

1619 and All That

It would be possible to write a biography of Malcolm X, saying only true things, that consisted of five chapters: his experiences as a drug dealer, his experiences as a numbers-runner, his experiences as a burglar, his experiences as a pimp...and then, after a spiritual awakening in prison, his experiences as a leader in an Afrocentric Muslim cult whose followers believe that white people were created by an evil black scientist named Yacub and that the world will be saved by the arrival of a spaceship carrying Allah—who will finally cleanse the world of white people and re-establish a black utopia on earth.

Likewise, it would be possible to write a history of America, saying only true things, that focused entirely on the cruelty of Indian populations toward European settlers and their descendants, citing broken treaties, kidnappings, and assorted massacres of white women and children.

Such books would be factually correct but would miss the forest for the trees since a fair and accurate, wide-angle view of Malcolm X's life cannot avoid the critical role he played in the civil rights movement of the mid-twentieth century, and a fair and accurate, wide-angle account of American history cannot avoid the genocidal upheavals visited upon Indians, intentionally and unintentionally, by European settlers and their descendants.

Saying true things, in other words, is not your *only* job if you're attempting to produce a fair and accurate account of the past. You also need to provide adequate historical context for the true things you are saying—or else you wind up distorting the account and ultimately leaving your readers less informed about the subject, and about the truth of what happened, even if they can rattle off a list of true things.

Providing adequate historical context becomes even more crucial if, at the end of your account, you're going to render moral judgment…which is the entire purpose of the *New York Times*'s controversial 1619 Project. It's revisionist history with an explicit moral imperative: to show how racism lurks behind every significant development in American history, from the earliest settlements to the last presidential election.

Lack of historical context is the most serious problem with the 1619 Project. It's not the only problem, by any means; as I'll discuss below, a core claim of the 1619 Project is flat out false. But lack of historical context is the *overriding and uncorrectable* flaw. Given that lack of context and false claims, the 1619 Project is ludicrously bad American history. *But so what?* As American histories go, is the 1619 Project more ludicrous than, say, Parson Weems's morally uplifting tales about young George Washington chopping down a cherry tree or the resolute general taking a knee with his troops at Valley Forge?[42] From the earliest days of the republic, more or less inaccurate American histories have been told and retold, and have tended, until relatively recently, to gloss over the country's worst moral failures. Thus, Nikole Hannah-Jones, director of the 1619 Project, sees her work as a corrective. She has said that her intention was not to produce an objective history; she doesn't believe such a thing is possible *or desirable*. Rather, her intention is to "reframe" American history. Let me quote her again, as I did in the introductory chapter of this book: "The fight here is about who gets to control the national narrative, and therefore, the nation's shared memory of itself."

This makes total sense...if you're a postmodern subjectivist. If there is no independent reality against which historical claims can be measured, and no requirement of logical consistency in methodology or logical coherence in presentation, then the way to push back against a dominant narrative is by creating a more powerful counternarrative. Not a *more accurate* counternarrative, but a *more powerful one*. Despite the lip service paid by the 1619 Project's advocates to teaching America's "true history," the de facto project of the Project is to replace one narrative with another, neither of which is more or less objectively true, since objective truth does not exist.

This would be extraordinarily cynical if those advocates understood what they were doing. Remember, however, that the 1619 Project is a Woke document. Thus, it is an offshoot of the subjectivist worldview that denies our intellects access to a universe beyond our own perceptions and the postmodernist twist on that worldview that rejects logic as an arbiter of truth. There is no reason to think that Nikole Hannah-Jones has a grasp of epistemological debates. She has said, "All of this inequality was constructed, so all of this inequality can be deconstructed"—which suggests she's tossing around the verb without knowing its origins or its standard academic use.[43] (To "deconstruct" inequality, in the literal, academic sense, would be to play around with the concept in order to show how the have-nots really have more than the haves.) But Hannah-Jones's Project, whether she realizes it or not, sits on pseudo-intellectual clouds; its *raison d'être*, which is to render a substantial moral judgment on American history, is therefore hopelessly compromised.

The fact that the 1619 Project is grounded in postmodern subjectivism, which is to say that it is grounded in neither reality nor reason, makes criticizing it for howling factual errors a fool's errand. If you've bought in, you've bought in the whole way; criticisms of it are naturally dismissed as evidence of bad faith. As Hannah-Jones has said, "I think we would not be being honest if we didn't say me being a black woman in particular, a black woman who looks and presents the way that I do, that I didn't get a certain, extremely vicious type of pushback."[44]

Curiously enough, being a black woman and looking and presenting the way that she does did not prevent the most prestigious newspaper in America from throwing its intellectual weight behind the project, nor from doubling down even in the face of withering, scrupulously documented criticism[45] from historians across the political spectrum.[46]

Still, if a black person *feels* victimized, she *is* victimized. Such are the rules of the road once you've bought in, once you're Woke. And today's *New York Times* is nothing if not Woke.

So, yes, it's a fool's errand to detail any particular howling factual error in the 1619 Project. But because the un-Woke masses are still answerable to reality and reason, a fool's errand is work that needs to be done. Central to the 1619 Project's thesis that racism is the explanation for every major development in American history is the editors' claim that the Revolutionary War was fought because colonial leaders feared that England was about to outlaw slavery in the colonies. The desire for independence from England was merely a pretext, or at best side benefit; the main impetus for the conflict was preservation of slavery. Despite their high talk about self-government, taxation without representation, and natural rights, what was *really* on the minds of Washington, Jefferson, Madison, Franklin, Adams, et al. was making sure that slave labor continued to power the colonial economies, north and south alike.

As Hannah-Jones writes in her lead essay for the 1619 Project:

> Conveniently left out of our founding mythology is the fact that one of the primary reasons some of the colonists decided to declare their independence from Britain was because they wanted to protect the institution of slavery. By 1776, Britain had grown deeply conflicted over its role in the barbaric institution that had reshaped the Western Hemisphere. In London, there were growing calls to abolish the slave trade. This would have upended the economy of the colonies, in both the North and the South. The wealth and prominence that allowed Jefferson, at just 33, and the other founding fathers to believe they could successfully break off from one of the mightiest empires in the world came from the dizzying profits generated by chattel slavery. In other

> words, we may never have revolted against Britain if some of the founders had not understood that slavery empowered them to do so; nor if they had not believed that independence was required in order to ensure that slavery would continue.[47]

Is she right? No. The preservation of slavery was decidedly *not* a significant concern among colonial leaders in the 1770s (not even "some of" them, as in Hannah-Jones's grudgingly, surreptitiously amended text cited above); the preservation of slavery was *not* a significant factor in their decision to break from England.[48] She has got that point dead wrong. As often happens with historical analyses, however, if you stare long and hard enough in just the right places, there's *almost-kind-of* something to see to suggest otherwise. For instance, there was the Somerset Decision of 1772. In that case, Lord Mansfield, a high court judge in England, freed a slave named James Somerset who had been purchased by an Englishman in Massachusetts and brought back to England—before Somerset could be re-sold and shipped to Jamaica. In his ruling, Mansfield memorably condemned the institution that had allowed Somerset to be bought and sold in the first place:

> A foreigner cannot be imprisoned here on the authority of any law existing in his own country: the power of a master over his servant is different in all countries, more or less limited or extensive; the exercise of it therefore must always be regulated by the laws of the place where exercised. The state of slavery is of such a

> nature, that it is incapable of now being introduced by Courts of Justice upon mere reasoning or inferences from any principles, natural or political; it must take its rise from positive law; the origin of it can in no country or age be traced back to any other source: immemorial usage preserves the memory of positive law long after all traces of the occasion, reason, authority, and time of its introduction are lost; and in a case so odious as the condition of slaves must be taken strictly, the power claimed by this return was never in use here; no master ever was allowed here to take a slave by force to be sold abroad because he had deserted from his service, or for any other reason whatever; we cannot say the cause set forth by this return is allowed or approved of by the laws of this kingdom, therefore the man must be discharged.[49]

What Lord Mansfield is arguing is that because slavery is an "odious" and *unnatural* institution, the only way to uphold the ownership claim of a slaveholder is if an explicit law has been enacted (a "positive law") to allow it. But no such law existed in England. Although there were slaves living in England at the time, and there were laws regulating the slave trade and treatment of slaves, there were no laws specifically instituting or banning slavery itself. Therefore, Mansfield reasons, Somerset must be freed, regardless of the law in place in the country where he'd initially been purchased. Only an explicit positive law can create an unnatural institution.

It was a bold ruling, a noble one. But did it have the effect that Hannah-Jones claims?

Not close. The Somerset Decision did not ban slavery in England, and Lord Mansfield himself acknowledged that different places will have different laws governing "the power of a master over his servant." Thus, he gave not the slightest indication that his judgment would be binding in North America, or for that matter in England's Caribbean colonies, where far more slaves were being held under British rule than in its thirteen North American colonies combined. If the thought of colonial abolition even occurred to Mansfield, there is no hint of that in his ruling. And although the ruling was cheered by the nascent abolitionist movement in England, led by Granville Sharp, that movement remained minuscule until well after the Revolutionary War. The Somerset Decision received barely a mention in the American press, and none of the leaders of the revolution—and we have reams and reams of their writings—seemed exercised over it.[50] It just wasn't a big deal on this side of the Atlantic.

Ironically, a far more substantial abolitionist movement was gathering at the time…in Pennsylvania among Quakers. Insisting, as Hannah-Jones does, that abolitionist spirit in England caused the southern colonies in North America to throw in their lot with the northern colonies is like saying that a whiff of a distant cigarette caused bystanders to dash headlong toward a fuming canister of tear gas.

The Somerset Decision, in other words, contributes next-to-nothing to the argument that the American colonies were moved to declare their independence in order to preserve slavery. But is there any other support for the case? Advocates for the 1619 Project often cite a 1775 proclamation issued by the royal governor of Virginia, the Earl of Dunmore, that established martial law in the colony and promised freedom to slaves who abandoned their plantations and joined the British forces. Except that's not quite what the Dunmore Proclamation promised; rather, it promised freedom *only to those slaves who were the property of rebels.* Slaveholders who stayed loyal to England were free to keep their slaves—and it's worth noting that Dunmore himself was an unrepentant slaveholder. The aim of the proclamation was to weaken England's *military enemies.* Even though the Declaration of Independence wasn't issued until July of the following year, the Battles of Lexington and Concord, and the Battle of Bunker Hill had already been fought in the North. English and American forces were already skirmishing up and down the Eastern Seaboard, not only in New England but in South Carolina and Virginia. (Hence, the proclamation's establishment of martial law in Virginia.)

Unlike Lord Mansfield three years earlier, Dunmore did get the attention of colonial slaveholders and pissed off many of them. But it mainly pissed off those who were already in rebellion. Dunmore's gambit, in other words, was an *effect* of the rebellion, not a *cause* of it. Consider that George Washington (himself, of course, a slaveholder) had taken command of the Continental Army *five months before* the Dunmore Proclamation.

Nevertheless, advocates for the 1619 Project continue to trot out Mansfield and Dunmore as evidence for their thesis. Hannah-Jones also likes to point out that Jefferson's original draft of the Declaration of Independence contained a passionately anti-slavery passage in which he charged that the King of England had "waged cruel war against human nature itself, violating its most sacred rights of life and liberty in the persons of distant people...captivating and carrying them into slavery in another hemisphere or to incur miserable death in their transportation thither."

That passage never made it into the final version of the Declaration. Why? Because, as Jefferson himself attested in his 1821 *Autobiography*, if he had kept that passage in the final version, representatives of Georgia and South Carolina would never have signed onto the document. Even "our Northern brethren," Jefferson wrote, "felt a little tender under these censures; for tho' their people have very few slaves themselves, yet they had been pretty considerable carriers of them to others."

Does this constitute an *aha!* moment?

Not if you give it a moment of thought. Indeed, it argues *against* the 1619 Project case. After all, what were Georgia and South Carolina going to do if Jefferson had refused to strike the passage? Remain loyal to England? But how can that be if their paramount concern was that England was about to abolish slavery? Fight England on their own? But that would have been suicidal. The very fact that there was a possibility of Georgia and South Carolina not signing the Declaration of Independence underscores how little their representatives were worried about the prospect of abolition being imposed on them by England.

For that matter, if English abolitionism posed an existential threat to the economic well-being of the American colonies, why did none of the Caribbean colonies, where slavery powered their *entire* economies, join the revolt against England? The answer, of course, is that English abolitionism posed no such threat. England itself was benefitting enormously from goods produced by slave labor and from the slave trade itself. The idea that the king and Parliament were about to end slavery in their overseas territorial possessions wasn't a blip on the intellectual radar of colonial leaders in the 1770s.

Let's not lose sight of this final point: we know what those colonial leaders were thinking. We have volumes of their public writings and private correspondence. English abolitionism wasn't a primary concern of anyone's. It wasn't a secondary or even a tertiary concern.

The claim that the Revolutionary War was, in any meaningful way, fought to preserve slavery is thus completely false. It is demonstrably false. Yet teachers in public schools across the United States are now dutifully informing their students that the Revolutionary War was fought to preserve slavery. Why? Because if a sufficient number of people become convinced that it's true, then it becomes true. Those are the rules of Woke subjectivism, remember? If you keep growing the discourse community, if you keep "doing the work," you reach critical mass. That's when the miracle happens. Falsehood transitions to truth. The keynote, indeed the *only* note, of the 1619 Project is that racism is the story behind every story. Every aspect of America's past and America's present, from the very inception of the United States to the headlines in this morning's paper, involves racial oppression. That is the gospel Hannah-Jones is preaching. Nothing significant happens that isn't race related. Nothing good. Nothing bad. Nothing indifferent. Racism is either in the foreground, or it's lurking in the background, if only we have eyes to see it.

Mythologies

The omnipresence and explanatory power of racism is, as I said earlier, the "theory" in Critical Race Theory. To call it a theory, however, is slightly misleading. It is less a theory than an *axiom*: the Critical Race Axiom. Grasping the theory-axiom distinction enables us to make sense of the various rhetorical approaches utilized by advocates of CRT. Axioms are more basic than theories. Theories are falsifiable beliefs that are logically analyzed and empirically tested to determine their validity. If a theory doesn't hold up, it's either revised or abandoned altogether. Axioms, on the other hand, are systemic starting points; they are methodological givens. They are not falsifiable once you've bought into the system, and thus there is never a need to revise them. They are not subject to logical analysis and empirical testing *because they are the tools of logical analysis and empirical testing.*

Theories are granted no such immunity. Logical analysis and empirical testing can undermine even a well-established theory. That's what happened when Isaac Newton's centuries old theories of universal gravitation and space-time ran afoul of Albert Einstein's theory of general relativity. Einstein's theory was confirmed in 1919 by a comparison of star positions during and after a solar eclipse; the test proved that light bent, as predicted by relativity—which necessitated a major overhaul of Newtonian theories. That's how the process works. Einstein had a theory, which was logically analyzed, empirically tested, and eventually confirmed. Confirmation of Einstein's theory *necessarily* undermined traditional theories of space, time, and gravitation put forward by Newton; Newton's theories had to be revised. Note, however, that nothing Einstein ever wrote or said called into question the *axioms* under which both he and

Newton operated. They were both reasoning the same way. The laws of noncontradiction and causality—which are the axioms of logic and testability—remained intact. (They still do, despite the occasional bleats from quantum physicists.)

If you take as axiomatic that racism lies at the heart of every significant event, then that's that. Your analysis of past and present events *must* go in that direction. You are not so much scrutinizing evidence as connecting the dots from the event to racism. *Here's what happened...now where's the racism?* That's the question that requires an answer. The causal role of racism is not a thing to be analyzed; it is the starting point from which the analysis proceeds.

Evidence that your axiom may be false, thus, represents not so much an intellectual challenge as a cognitive disconnect. It's not on the explanatory menu; it doesn't compute. For a critical race theorist, there is simply no way to process the suggestion that racism has no relation to a historical or current event. It's a non-starter. Because you're treading on an axiom rather than an actual theory, logical analysis and empirical testability become moot. What remains is emotion. And the emotional stakes are ratcheted up when the event is something the critical race theorist doesn't like.

For example, when the police kill a black man.

The murder of George Floyd, a black man, on May 25, 2020, by Derek Chauvin, a white police officer, captured the interest of the American public like no crime since the murder of Nicole Brown Simpson a quarter century earlier. Floyd's death was a clear case of a cop methodically killing a defenseless black man; it wasn't a sudden confrontation that went bad. Whatever Floyd's criminal history, whatever resistance to arrest

Floyd offered before being subdued, Chauvin knelt on his neck for over nine minutes, ignoring Floyd's pleas that he couldn't breathe, then ignoring the fact that Floyd had lost consciousness. Floyd was in Chauvin's custody; he was therefore, as the saying goes, in his care. Chauvin's actions were sickening and sadistic, as clear a case of police brutality as you'll ever witness. He was rightly convicted of second- and third-degree murder.

But were Chauvin's actions *racist*? Is there even the slightest reason to believe that Floyd's ethnicity influenced how Chauvin treated him? More broadly, is there the slightest reason to believe that racism factored into the confrontation between the police and Floyd that fateful day?

Not based on the evidence presented at Chauvin's murder trial.

Racism never came up in the prosecution's case.

As *National Review* columnist and former federal prosecutor Andrew McCarthy has noted, the police neither hunted down nor randomly stopped Floyd.[51] They crossed paths with him only because they had been called by an employee at a local market, Cup Foods. Floyd had passed a cashier—a young black man, for what it's worth—a counterfeit twenty-dollar bill. If the cashier hadn't reported Floyd to the store manager, the twenty dollars would have come out of the cashier's own pocket. Afterward, several employees, including the cashier, pleaded with Floyd, whose Mercedes-Benz SUV remained parked across the street, to return to the market and square things. Floyd, sitting behind the steering wheel in a meth- and fentanyl-induced haze, refused. Sitting next to Floyd in the front seat was a drug dealer named Maurice Hall; sitting in the back seat was Floyd's friend, Shawanda Hill. Floyd was planning to drive her home.

Only after Floyd refused to pay what he owed at the market were the police called. Once the police arrived, what were they supposed to do? There was no chance that Floyd wasn't going to be arrested. Again, here's McCarthy:

> This simply was not, as the conventional narrative holds, a case of police overreacting to a trivial counterfeiting violation (and by the way, passing false currency is a crime under federal and state law). The police got involved because of a citizen complaint, they investigated because there was evidence of a counterfeiting crime, and Floyd's impaired condition rendered it inconceivable that they would have just written him a ticket and let him drive away.[52]

For the sake of the public's safety, therefore, as well as his own, Floyd was going to be arrested. Unsurprisingly, he had a strong preference not to be arrested. The rest of the story is well known. As for Chauvin, McCarthy points out: "Not a shred of evidence was introduced at the trial that Derek Chauvin is a racist. None. There was nothing in the weeks of testimony that even hinted at such a thing. The prosecutors who aggressively urged the jury to convict Chauvin of murder never intimated that racism played any role in the crimes. They convincingly argued that he was a bad cop, not a racist cop."[53]

Then, in a final ironic twist, when *federal prosecutors*, at the direction of President Biden's Department of Justice, charged the already-convicted Chauvin with violating Floyd's civil rights, Chauvin jumped at the chance to plead guilty—copping to a civil rights violation, which casual observers wrongly interpret as a confession of racist motivation—in exchange for serving out his federal and state sentences concurrently, and doing his time in federal custody rather than at a harsher, maximum-security state prison in Minnesota, where the crime was committed.[54]

It was win-win. Chauvin gets no extra time, a nicer prison cell, and more privileges while he's behind bars, and the Biden DOJ gets to crow about bringing the hammer down on a racist. Except, again, *no evidence of Chauvin's racism was ever presented in court.*

How is it possible that racism had nothing to do with the incident that galvanized the demand for "racial justice" across the United States?

To the critical race theorist, it's a non-question: even if there's no evidence that racism inspired the initial call to the police, even if there's no evidence that racism influenced the actions of the police, even if no evidence of racism was mentioned during the trial, racism nevertheless explains what happened to George Floyd. Because it's not the individuals. It's the system. Derek Chauvin knelt on George Floyd's neck until he was dead. But Derek Chauvin was only the instrument of his murder. George Floyd's actual murderer was systemic racism. It was the United States that was kneeling on George Floyd's neck.

How?

Well, you see, the first enslaved Africans arrived in America in 1619, and slave labor built the early American economy, and the United States itself only came into existence because colonial slaveholders were terrified England was going to abolish slavery, and then came the Three-Fifths Compromise, and fugitive slave laws, and the Dred Scott decision, and the Draft Riots, and the rise of the Ku Klux Klan, and Jim Crow, and the Tulsa Massacre, and the Scottsboro Boys, and the Tuskegee Experiment, and redlining, and Emmett Till, and Bull Connor, and the Baptist Street Church bombing, and white flight, and the education gap, and the wealth gap, and hands-up-don't-shoot, and that pretty much covers American history, so of course racism killed George Floyd.

Yes, but in this particular case, there's no evidence of—

Look, I know what happened to George Floyd, and you know what happened to George Floyd. Both of us know that his murder fits a well-established pattern of the police reflexively using lethal force against black suspects. That's the racist system under which we live. George Floyd is another black man killed by systemic racism. That's my truth, and if you weren't a racist, it would be your truth too.

But isn't that—

Do the work!

Curious catchphrase, "Do the work!" Among the Woke, it's taken to mean something like, "Learn about the reality of oppression around you!" Let me suggest another way to hear it, however: doing the work means prioritizing personal narrative over evidence and logic, and valuing the testimony of members of historically marginalized communities over objective analysis. Take, for example, the aforesaid well-established pattern of the police reflexively using lethal force against black suspects. It turns out that that pattern doesn't exist. That was the conclusion of a 2016 study by Harvard economist Roland Fryer.[55] It wasn't what Fryer set out to show; it wasn't what he was expecting to find. He called the result, based on meticulously gathered, peer-reviewed data, the most shocking of his academic career. Yet that was what the data revealed: if you control for frequency of interactions—that is, if you take into account the fact that black people are far more likely, per capita, to be contacted by cops—you find that the police are no more likely to use lethal force against black suspects than against white suspects.

But doesn't the fact that black people are far more likely to be contacted by cops prove systemic racism?

No, it doesn't. Not if you give the question a moment's thought. The police go where street crime is. That's their job. That's what we *want* them to do. That's where we *want* them to be. If there is more street crime in black neighborhoods than in white neighborhoods, we *want* more cops in those black neighborhoods for the sake of the law-abiding residents. If most of the street criminals in those neighborhoods are black, we *want* the cops to stop them more often…again, for the sake of the law-abiding residents. The police are not instruments in the performance of social equity. They are instruments in the maintenance of public safety. You realize that as soon as you remove race from the equation. The police also contact male suspects far more often than they contact female suspects; indeed, the male-female contact disparity is much greater than the black-white disparity. Can we infer from the male-female disparity that the police are biased against men? Of course not. Cops contact male suspects far more often than female suspects because men commit far more street crime than women do.

Whatever may be said about America's sordid racialized past and the socioeconomic factors that underlie street crime, the unfortunate reality is that *at this moment* black people commit a vastly disproportionate share of street crime. For that reason, and for that reason alone, they will *necessarily* be contacted by the police more than other ethnic groups.

Fryer's results, as you may imagine, did not sit well among CRT apologists. Margaret Kimberley, co-founder and senior columnist at the *Black Agenda Report*, called him "a traitor, a Quisling, the worst sort of Uncle Tom."[56] His transgression, of course, was to set empirical evidence over collective belief, verifiability over strong, in-group feelings. Two years before Fryer made his findings public, two law school professors had warned critical race theorists of the perils of reliance on the traditional methodologies of social science:

> ...a collaboration between CRT and social science risks undermining CRT critiques of objectivity and neutrality and potentially limits the theory's ability to combat structural forms of racial inequality. CRT scholars can mitigate these risks by choosing social science methods carefully and by recognizing that social science is only one among several modes of knowledge production.[57]

It's a classic heads-I-win/tails-you-lose scenario. When the methods of social science reveal what the CRT scholar expects to discover, they are valid; when they contradict his expectations, when they undermine the narratives to which he is committed, the methods must be called into question. On the one hand, objectivity and neutrality "can provide CRT with data and theoretical frameworks to support key empirical claims."[58] On the other hand, CRT instructs us that objectivity and neutrality are intellectual ruses in the service of white supremacy.

Fryer's work landed squarely on the other hand.

The revelation that cops are no more likely to use lethal force against black suspects than against white suspects wasn't the only eye-opener to emerge from the Fryer study. Fryer also found that the police were 50 percent *more likely* to use *non-lethal* force against black suspects. Cops, in other words, were more likely to rough up black suspects than white suspects, yet no more likely to kill them.

Taken together, the two findings are confounding—particularly if you're arguing that racism, loosely defined, is at work. How can it be that cops are racially biased at first, when they're confronting black suspects, yet their racism seems to evaporate as tensions rise in confrontations? How can it be that the cops are bigots when they shove, but not bigots when they shoot?

One possible explanation comes from an observation made by Columbia linguistics professor and social critic John McWhorter about racial authenticity. McWhorter notes, "…in the Black community, there is a value placed on being a badass motherfucker. Some of this is that a critical mass of people salutes these men for the resistance, the idea being that that's the Black thing. You don't put up with any shit."[59]

If McWhorter's badass motherfucker hypothesis is correct, it becomes much easier to understand why black suspects, and in particular young black men, might feel personally obliged, and perhaps socially conditioned, to be noncooperative when they are stopped, detained, and questioned by the police. Here's McWhorter: "But then it comes out with this business of resisting arrest and people saluting; it is an indication of your masculinity, that you're kind of saluting Black oppression in the past."[60] From the perspective of the police, however, it makes no difference whether a suspect is being noncompliant due to cultural conditioning, or out of a sense that he's combating a system of past and present injustices, or simply because he's being a dick. Cops are trained to use gradually escalating force in order to obtain compliance. If you don't promptly comply with a lawful police command, regardless of your ethnicity, you are going to get shoved, you are going to get spun, you are going to get wrestled to the ground. If black suspects are consistently less likely to comply, they are consistently more likely to be manhandled.

But *not* more likely to be killed, according to Fryer's study.

The Rigged Game

The proposition that the United States is systemically racist is, as I've attempted to show, either untrue or unclear. To be charitable, let's suppose it's the latter. What is required, in that case, is not dismissal but clarification. Reasonable acknowledgments should be made about the lingering effects of America's racialized past. No, Americans did not invent the African slave trade; Africans were being rounded up and sold by Muslim slavers for half a millennium before Columbus set sail to the New World. (The Spanish and Portuguese, who inaugurated the trans-Atlantic slave trade, likely picked up the idea from the Muslims who conquered and ruled the Iberian Peninsula for centuries before being driven out during that pivotal year of 1492.) But, yes, even if the buying and selling of Africans long preceded the English settlement of North America, and even if thousands of slave ships carried millions of slaves to misery, degradation, and death before such a thing as "the United States" was ever conceived, the United States profited more from the peculiar institution than any current world power. The psychic justification for African slavery, segregation, and the various forms of oppression that followed was always a belief in the intellectual and moral inferiority of black people. Clearly, then, the United States has a *legacy* of anti-black racism, and that legacy continues to play itself out, notwithstanding the race-neutrality of the systems by which our federal, state, and local governments now operate. We're still awash in intellectual and moral disparities, concrete, easily measurable disparities, that stubbornly track antiquated and biologically dubious racial dividing lines.

Even worse, those stubborn disparities seem to have broken the will of large swaths of America's black population, who have embraced a culture of perpetual grievance, based on a belief in their perpetual victimization—a pathological culture in which intellectual and moral failures become badges of racial authenticity. Poor black families are in a ruinous state, with three-quarters of black children born out of wedlock and more than half living in single-parent households. The phrase "baby daddy" has no stigma in that culture; on the contrary, it has eclipsed "husband" in common usage.

You can debate the weight of various causes of this collective disaster. Surely, racism directed against their ancestors placed many generations of black Americans behind the eight ball at birth; surely, too, their own lifestyle choices, including their rejection of middle class cultural norms as "acting white," keeps many black Americans behind the eight ball and transmits their behind-the-eight-ball positioning to children. You can also debate whether government efforts to remedy the disaster have, on the whole, tended to alleviate or exacerbate it. The point here is not to argue policy; the point, rather, is to observe that virtually every self-destructive behavior known to man is found disproportionately among children raised in broken homes. (Which is why the phrase "broken home" is preferable to its cozier alternatives.) If the collapse of the black family can be traced to America's history of slavery, segregation, and consequent black poverty—and that's surely a plausible thesis—then it's fair to say that the legacy of anti-black racism is indeed *systemically* present. If "systemic racism" means that, and only that, then there's truth in the proposition that the United States is systemically racist.

Past racism plays out systemically, even if the systems themselves are race-neutral.

That acknowledgment *might* be common ground for CRT advocates and opponents.

But even if it were a consensus view, even if it gained universal assent, where do you go from there? Suppose, as a thought experiment, that absolutely everyone agreed that kids raised in single-parent homes are disadvantaged in crucial ways, and because a majority of black kids are so situated, they are, in effect, born disadvantaged. Suppose, further, that absolutely everyone agreed, as CRT advocates insist, that self-destructive life choices should *never* be laid at the feet of black people, that the very notion of "self-destructive life choices," with respect to child-rearing, is essentially racist. Remember, here, that chart from the Smithsonian's National Museum of African American History and Culture in which delaying gratification, planning for the future, and idealizing a family unit of a father, mother, and children are indicators of white supremacist culture. Suppose that absolutely everyone, in our thought experiment, is agreed. Systemic racism is to blame for the socioeconomic stagnation of black people....

Now what?

The history remains the history; it cannot be retroactively fixed. Personal choices are personal choices; among the rights safeguarded by the Constitution, unmentioned but undisputed, is the right to screw up your long-term socioeconomic prospects—and even, in the case of black people, to evolve a culture of racial authenticity in which screwing up your long-term socioeconomic prospects is the blackest thing you can do.

How do you break the cycle? How is racial equity achieved? With cash reparations? But consider the logic: the historical mistreatment of their ancestors has so weakened and deformed the agency of black people that they cannot be expected to make decisions in their long-term socioeconomic interests... so let's dump a sack of money on their doorstep. Is that a workable solution?

Yet there is an even deeper problem with idea of reparations. It is an *essentially* white solution. That is, it assumes that with enough wealth redistribution, you can return everyone to something like a fair starting position. Whatever happens thereafter, the thinking goes, will also be fair since no one will have a leg up. Game on!

The problem, however, is that the game is still the same. Capitalism. Competition. Winners and losers. Why is that a problem? Let's return, yet again, to that Smithsonian chart: *Hard work is the key to success. Work before play. Heavy value on the ownership of goods, space, property. Follow rigid time scales. Be polite.* These, according to the National Museum of African American History and Culture, are signatures of white supremacist culture. They're also indisputably building blocks for success in a capitalist system. If you accept the essentialist tenets of CRT, black people will *always* be disadvantaged under capitalism. Even if you can return everyone to a fair starting position, inequities will necessarily emerge...and owing to the essential differences between black and white people, those inequities will favor white people. Capitalism is not a system designed for the realization of the full potential of black people. No matter how many times you shuffle the deck, the cards are still marked. The game is rigged. There's a reason Kimberlé Crenshaw cites Marxist thought as one of the wellsprings for CRT.

Which brings us to a final point about CRT. The names most often associated with its origins are Crenshaw, Derrick Bell, and Richard Delgado—legal scholars who formulated its basic framework from the late 1970s through the mid-1990s. But there is another name that should be mentioned, a name typically omitted from CRT discussions, the black sheep, so to speak, of CRT, though a more appropriate title may be its absentee father: Leonard Jeffries.

Jeffries is a formerly notorious but now mostly forgotten academic carnival barker initially hired to teach political science at City College of New York in 1969. He soon moved to San Jose State College, where he founded its Black Studies Department, then returned to CCNY in 1972 to organize its own Black Studies Department. From his post as Chair of Black Studies at CCNY, and largely out of the public eye, Jeffries spun out crackpot racial theories in which greater concentrations of melanin allowed black people, whom he called "sun people" to "negotiate the vibrations of the universe"; white people, whom he called "ice people," did not have enough melanin to tap into those universal vibrations, so in order to survive, they had to become more individualistic, competitive, and exploitative.[61] Sun people, according to Jeffries, "have had the beginning of the march of humankind. We are the mothers and fathers of civilization. We developed science, mathematics, and philosophy. And we stand on that." What ice people had going for them was that they were greedier, crueler, and more devious in their methods and actions. Ice people were thus able to rob sun people of their intellectual heritage and pride of place in the civilizational march. "So how the hell can you be beating on us about our self-esteem?" Jeffries inquires,

> Particularly when in the culture of white racism, there is such a negative image of African people? Feel-good curriculum. What the hell do you think the existing curriculum is? We learn about Washington and the cherry tree. I don't want to hear nothing about Washington and the cherry tree. I don't want to feel good or feel bad about Washington. I want to know about Washington and the enslavement process. I don't want to know about Jefferson and his Declaration of Independence in 1776. Let me know about first draft in 1775 when he compromised and took out the indictment against slavery. And then let me know some more about Jefferson, his character and whatnot.[62]

Sound familiar?

Here's more of Professor Jeffries's scholarship, from that same 1991 speech at Empire State Black Arts and Cultural Festival in Albany, New York:

> Ice and sun are very real and very scientific. We are sun people, people of color because of the sun. The melanin factor. Europeans have a lack of melanin and have lost a great deal of it because much of the European development has been in the caves of Europe where you do not need melanin. So the factor of the ice is a key factor in the development of the European biologically, culturally, economically, socially. And what we are talking about is the values that are transmitted from ecologies....[63]

Leonard Jeffries is what CRT's racial essentialism sounds like once you peel away the postmodernist flourishes, heave-ho the crypto-Marxist cant, and start to say in ordinary language what you mean. White people were able to overcome and subjugate black people, notwithstanding black people's elevated cognitive skills, because white people are innately sneakier and meaner. Capitalism rewards sneakiness and meanness. By their very nature, therefore, white people will always have a leg up in a competitive, capitalist system. It's organized around what they do well.

What's the main obstacle to black people's socioeconomic progress America? Their niceness. Their easygoingness. Their generosity. Their devotion to communal well-being even at the expense of self-interest. Their natural reluctance to claim ownership of ideas or worldly things.

The main difference between today's critical race theorists and Professor Jeffries is that he said the quiet part out loud.

Critical Race Theory, if you strip it down to its essence, is a desperate but ultimately transparent exercise in special pleading. Fuzzy concepts such as systemic racism, bigoted fictions such as racial essentialism, and clownish methodologies like deconstruction permit CRT advocates to skirt painful realities about the underachievement of recent generations of black Americans.

You can sympathize with the endeavor. But it won't work. The realities are there. You cannot "theorize" your way around them, despite the persistent, sometimes combative efforts by critical race theorists to do so. You cannot lard over verifiable evidence with subjective narratives and essentialist epistemologies; you cannot twist, torture, and remake logic into a froggy, free-associative, self-contradictory haze. You may achieve a few short-term objectives. You may scare the gibberish out of the palefaces in the faculty lounge and intimidate the suits on the corporate board. You may get a Center for Social Justice here, a Diversity, Equity, and Inclusion Officer there. Wealthy societies will bankroll the occasional Ministry of Silly Walks.[64] Time, however, is a theoretical corrosive. Future generations will figure out what you've done.

CHAPTER THREE

#Me-Also

Believe Women (Sometimes)

Tara Reade now qualifies as a footnote to history. But for several weeks during the spring of 2020, as Democrats were selecting their nominee to run against Donald Trump, Reade roiled the US presidential race. Former Vice President Joe Biden was by then the clear front-runner for the nomination. So there was significant hand-wringing when Reade claimed that in 1993, when she was a junior staffer in Biden's office, he'd shoved her against a wall in the basement of a building, forcibly kissed her, slid his fingers underneath her clothes, and penetrated her vagina. After she pulled away, according to Reade, Biden looked shocked and said, "Come on, man, I heard you liked me." Moments later, he added, "You're nothing to me, nothing," but then he clasped her shoulders and said, "You're okay, you're fine."[65]

Once Biden walked off, Reade rushed to the restroom to collect herself, then, sobbing, headed home. She told her mother, her brother, and a close friend what had happened. Her mother advised her to file a police report. Rather than go that route, Reade complained to Biden's executive assistant and two of his senior aides. Nothing happened. She filed a written complaint with the Senate Personnel Office. Again, no action against Biden was taken. Soon afterward, however, she was stripped of most of her duties and reassigned to an office without a window. Finally, she was advised by one of the senior Biden aides to whom she'd complained that she was no longer a good fit for the staff and was given a month to find another job. She didn't find one, and she never worked in DC again.

That was Reade's story.

Biden, who had a richly documented history of awkward and unwanted hair sniffing, hugging, and shoulder massaging of young women, adamantly denied that the incident with Reade took place. The members of his staff to whom Reade said she'd complained also denied her accusations, and no record of her written complaint to the Senate Personnel Office could be found.

On the other hand, Reade's brother came forward to confirm that she'd told him about the incident. So did two of Reade's friends; one said that she'd told her about an incident with Biden around the time it occurred; the other said that Reade had told her about it in 2008. Reade's mom, whom Reade said was the first person she'd told, was deceased by the time the story broke in 2020. But Reade claimed that her mom had once mentioned the incident on-air during a call-in segment of CNN's *Larry King Live* about the toxic workplace culture in Washington. Sure enough, a tape was dug up from an August 11, 1993, episode of the program—five days after Reade was fired—in which a caller from San Luis Obispo, California, where Reade's mom resided, asks: "I'm wondering what a staffer would do besides go to the press in Washington? My daughter has just left there, after working for a prominent senator, and could not get through with her problems at all, and the only thing she could have done was go to the press, and she chose not to do it out of respect for him."[66]

Reade is certain that the caller was her mother.

As details of Reade's accusations broke, the press zeroed in on Reade's credibility. It discovered inconsistencies in Reade's account. The specific charge that Biden had digitally penetrated her was a later addition to a story she'd been recounting in blog posts since 2019. She was also unclear about the number of people she'd told; her brother, a diehard supporter of Biden's rival Bernie Sanders, was not on her initial list. Even in the Larry King transcript, it should be noted that Reade's mom refers only vaguely to "problems." If you're talking to a CNN producer, hoping to get on the air during a national call-in show, why be vague when the phrase "sexual assault" will vault you to the front of the line? And what are we to make of Reade's mom saying that her daughter declined to publicize that incident "out of respect" for the senator?

Reade insisted that she had tried to come forward with her story earlier, only to be ignored, and records show that she had in fact spoken to the *New York Times*, the *Washington Post*, *Vox*, and the Associated Press. But in none of those interviews had she mentioned a sexual assault. In her interview with AP, she explicitly denied that Biden's advances toward her constituted "sexual misconduct."

Further investigation revealed that Reade had claimed to be physically and/or sexually abused by at least four other people, including her dead father. She also had a dog in the fight for the Democratic nomination. Like her brother, she was staunchly pro-Sanders, and she had tweeted her rage as Biden began to pull ahead of Bernie in the early Democratic primaries.

So what are we to make of Tara Reade's accusations?

Was there enough evidence for a responsible district attorney to indict Joe Biden for sexual assault? Not unless he wanted to get his butt handed to him at trial. Reasonable doubt cries out from a half dozen directions. What about a civil suit? Could Reade have prevailed in a trial decided by a preponderance of the evidence? It's not out of the question, but it feels like a long shot.

Biden, of course, rode out the mini-crisis and wound up the forty-sixth president of the United States.

Whatever else may be said for or against Tara Reade's claims against Joe Biden, we can say one thing for certain: she has made the acquaintance of the man she accused of sexual assault. Government records demonstrate that they worked in the same office. Coworkers can place the two of them together under one roof. She and Biden really and truly know one another.

The same cannot be said about Christine Blasey Ford and Supreme Court Justice Brett Kavanaugh. There remains, as of this writing, no proof that the two of them have ever met. None. Not a hint. Not a whisper. Not a Higgs boson of objective, verifiable evidence. Note: I'm not talking about proof that he sexually assaulted her. I'm talking about proof that they have met. Yes, they had mutual friends. But had the two of them ever been in the same place at the same time? We know that on

September 27, 2018, Ford testified before the Senate Judiciary Committee, and the rest of the world, about a horrific ordeal that she suffered at the hands of Kavanaugh. But absolutely nothing apart from the words of her allegation against him puts the two of them together. It is imperative to let that sink in. Ford cannot show that she and the man she famously accused of sexual violence thirty-four or thirty-six years earlier, when they were teenagers, have ever been in the same place at the same time, let alone that he ever laid a hand on her.

The Ford-Kavanaugh scandal—and it *is* a scandal, though not for the reasons typically given—is often referred to as a case of he said/she said. That's false. It's a case of she said/he recoiled in shock and horror. *He apparently had no idea who she was or what she was talking about.* Nor was Ford able to jog his memory since she couldn't say where the assault occurred, except that it was at a house somewhere in the vicinity of Chevy Chase and Bethesda in Maryland, near a country club she and her friends frequented; nor could she say when the assault occurred, except that it was 1982, though maybe 1984; nor could she say how she got to the house where she was supposedly assaulted, or how she got back to her parents' house after she was assaulted, a twenty-minute drive from the country club, and therefore not within walking distance. Every witness to the incident whom she named denied it happened—including Ford's lifelong friend, Leland Keyser. About Leland Keyser: initially, she said only that she had no recollection of the incident. Which is strange. You'd think she'd have at least a flicker of a memory since, if Ford's account is accurate, once Ford fled the house after being assaulted, and was magically transported home, Keyser would have been left alone with three drunken, rapey teenage boys. Perhaps that realization is what led Keyser to amend her initial hedge that she had no recollection of the incident. She now states flatly, "I don't have any confidence in [Ford's] story." But she goes further. Ford's account, according to Keyser, "just didn't make any sense."[67]

No, it didn't. No, it doesn't.

During her testimony before the Senate Judiciary Committee, Ford explained her reason for coming forward: "I thought it was my civic duty to relay the information I had about Mr. Kavanaugh's conduct so that those considering his potential nomination would know about the assault."

The problem is that Ford herself doesn't *know* about the assault. She *believes* that Kavanaugh assaulted her, and there's no reason to think that her belief is insincere. Indeed, her belief may be unfalsifiable. But it is still just a belief. To believe something and to know something are different mental states. Knowledge is a specific kind of belief: it is *adequately justified true belief*. Ford's belief that Kavanaugh assaulted her is not merely inadequately justified; any fair analysis of the testimony she gave before the Senate Judiciary Committee suggests that her belief is *un*justified.

She can repeat over and over that she knows Kavanaugh assaulted her. But repetition has no alchemic power; it cannot change her belief into knowledge. Belief becomes knowledge only when it is adequately justified and true. Nothing Ford has ever said in public, and not a single piece of verifiable evidence, has moved the belief-knowledge needle even an inch to the right.

Nor can it be a thought crime to make that observation. It cannot be the case, and we *know* from Tara Reade's experience that it isn't, that a woman's claim of sexual assault is sacrosanct. Neither the moral seriousness of a claim, nor the criminal conduct it alleges, renders it immune from evidentiary demands and logical scrutiny. These, on the contrary, should intensify those demands and scrutiny. Recall Leland Keyser's words: Ford's account of her sexual assault by Brett Kavanaugh *doesn't make any sense.*

There is no objective reason to think that it happened.

Ford's supporters point to her therapist's notes from a May 2012 couples counseling session she and her husband attended. The notes have never been made public, but a portion of them were shown to a journalist at the *Washington Post*, who reported that although Kavanaugh isn't mentioned by name, Ford does indeed say that decades earlier she had been attacked by students from a prestigious boys' school—a description that fits Kavanaugh (as well as hundreds of other boys in the vicinity at the time). But even if Ford *had* mentioned Kavanaugh by name, and even if there were no inconsistencies between the details in her therapist's notes and the account of the attack that she provided to the Judiciary Committee (there are several inconsistencies), the notes themselves would only be evidence that Ford *sincerely believes* that Kavanaugh assaulted her, that she's not consciously lying. They would not be evidence that the assault happened.

Truth, I reiterate, is a correspondence between what you think and a reality that exists independently from what you think. You arrive at truth by adjusting what you think to reality, not by expecting reality to adjust to what you think. Because reality doesn't budge. And *in reality*, there are holes in Ford's account of the evening of her alleged sexual assault through which you can drive a nonexistent Uber taxi summoned by a nonexistent smartphone.

Let me put the matter in perspective. Nine black teenagers, who came to be known as the Scottsboro Boys, were infamously, unfairly, and falsely accused of raping two white women on a train in Alabama in 1931. No reasonable person now disputes that those nine young men were victims of a grotesque miscarriage of justice. Yet there was more objective evidence against them than has ever been brought against Brett Kavanaugh.

You may not like that analogy. You may not like the idea of casting a prominent, well-to-do white man who now sits on the United States Supreme Court as the victim of a gross injustice. But *like* has got nothing to do with it.

That's the reality.

Credibility and Desire

It must be noted that Ford wasn't the only woman to accuse Kavanaugh of sexual misconduct. Once her claims made the news, other women came forward. First in line was Deborah Ramirez, who recounted a lewd story about Kavanaugh waving his penis around at a booze-drenched Yale dormitory party. Next came Julie Swetnick, who insisted that she had observed Kavanaugh waiting his turn at a pre-arranged gang rape in a quiet residential neighborhood in Maryland. Ramirez and Swetnick opened the floodgates. Their accusations were reported breathlessly and credulously by mainstream news organizations, and the FBI was thereafter bombarded with tales of Kavanaugh's sexual escapades. Apparently, unbeknownst to his family and close friends, and going back decades, Kavanaugh had been living a life culled from the wildest wet dreams of Hugh Hefner, Keith Richards, and the Marquis de Sade. These accusations were not, by and large, the intimate variety. Logically, they should have produced hundreds of witnesses. Yet not a single witness has ever corroborated even one accusation against the man.

That didn't stop Ford's lawyer, Debra Katz, from insisting, "In the aftermath of these hearings, I believe that Christine's testimony brought about more good than the harm misogynist Republicans caused by allowing Kavanaugh on the court. He will always have an asterisk next to his name. When he takes a scalpel to *Roe v. Wade*, we will know who he is, we know his character, and we know what motivates him, and that is important; it is important that we know, *and that is part of what motivated Christine.*"[68] (Emphasis added.)

Nor did it stop Jason Johnson, a professor of communication and journalism, from ejaculating on MSNBC, "I've never heard of a guy who's a one-time rapist. I've never heard of a guy who's a one-time sexual assaulter. I grew up with guys like [Kavanaugh]. He's from around this area. He's the fifth guy at a gang rape."[69]

Katz's quasi-confession can be written off as a slip of the tongue, Johnson's slanderous bluster as mere clickbait (though it raises the obvious question of how many times Johnson has been the sixth guy at a gang rape in order to detect the telltale attributes of the fifth guy). More troubling is a matter-of-fact declaration by the National Women's Law Center, *three years after the Ford and Kavanaugh testimonies*: "Kavanaugh was confirmed to a lifetime position on the Supreme Court, despite being credibly accused by multiple women of sexual assault."[70]

The key word there is *credibly*.

What does "credibly" mean in this context? It is true that Kavanaugh has been accused by multiple women of sexual assault. It is also true that none of those accusations, in themselves, are credible—if credibility involves anything like an objective standard of evidentiary weight and logical consistency. Set aside the particulars of the case against Kavanaugh. If Jane accuses Joe, with whom she's had a verifiable relationship, of sexual misconduct, and then Mary, who also has had a verifiable relationship with Joe, makes a similar accusation, and then Sue, who also has had a verifiable relationship with Joe, makes a similar accusation, the three accusations support one another; their number lends to their collective credibility. On the other hand, if none of them has ever had a relationship with Joe, and none can provide the slightest evidence that the misconduct occurred, even though each of their accusations would, if true, involve multiple witnesses, and if, moreover, there is no record of sexual misconduct in Joe's past, then the three accusations do not support each other. Quite the reverse, they undermine each other. They suggest not that Joe has a track record of sexual misconduct but that at least three women are out to get Joe. You cannot get from multiplicity to credibility without meeting a minimal evidentiary and logical threshold in each case. Credibility must be rooted in something objective and verifiable.

But of course the adverb "credibly," as it is being used by the National Women's Law Center, *isn't* an objective standard. It's an altogether subjective state, a gut feeling, something akin to, "in a way that sounds believable to me." That's fine. Maybe Kavanaugh *seems like the type* to do those sorts of things. It's a form of bias, but there's nothing very worrisome about it. Bias is an inescapable feature of human nature, which means it's something that needs to be taken into account in the formulation of a rational judgment.

Recognizing the potential for bias, however, requires opening another line of inquiry: Is there anything in *your* background that would predispose you to judge him unfairly? Do you have anything to gain from it? Is there a personal or political motive at play?

In the case of Kavanaugh, such questions are especially pertinent. To ignore them is an act of bad faith. Supreme Court nominations are now second only to presidential elections in their contentiousness, and presidential campaigns themselves are significantly intensified by the prospect that the winner may wind up nominating one or more Supreme Court justices. Alexander Hamilton said of the judiciary branch that it was "beyond comparison the weakest of the three departments of power."[71] But a great deal of political power has been informally delegated to the Court, mostly through the eagerness of elected officials to dance around socially explosive issues such as gay marriage, gun rights, and, above all, abortion.

I said earlier that the Ford-Kavanaugh dustup was a scandal, but not for the reasons typically given. By the time the full Senate voted to confirm Kavanaugh to the Supreme Court, more Americans believed Ford's accusation against him than believed Kavanaugh's denial.[72]

That's the scandal.

It is sad, though not scandalous, that a traumatized and confused woman was ushered onto the national stage in a futile attempt to derail the nomination of an obviously qualified candidate for the Court, and that other women, with even more far-fetched stories, followed in her wake. But we live in politically charged times, and when you're the minority party, as Democrats were at the time, you occasionally play hardball to exert your will. It's undignified, to be sure, and the spectacle of members of the Senate Judiciary Committee poring over the puerile jottings of Kavanaugh's high school yearbook is no one's idea of statesmanship. But it's also par for the course in our current hyper-politicized res publica. The true scandal was that so many of us got bamboozled by the Democrats' shabby and transparent efforts to baselessly smear and taint the nominee. Yes, in the end, Kavanaugh joined the Court, but large portions of the American public came away from the hearings convinced that he was a sexual predator.

It's not Kavanaugh's scandal, or Ford's scandal, or even the Democrats' scandal.

It's *our* scandal.

There is no *reasonable* scenario in which the alleged assault happened the way Ford described it, or in which the incidents described by the other women happened at all, which means there is no *logical* cause to believe any of them. Due process, which applies not only in a courtroom but in any formal airing of grievances, requires that the burden of proof fall to the accuser. Even if that were not so, however, the only *objective* conclusion to draw from the fact patterns made public during the Kavanaugh confirmation hearing (or any time since) is that Kavanaugh did not assault, harass, or in any way bother Ford or any of his other accusers.

Note, however, the italicized adjectives: *Reasonable. Logical. Objective.*

What if those are no longer the qualities by which disputes are settled?

What if they're no longer habits of mind to be cultivated and celebrated?

What if their cultivation and celebration is discriminatory against women?

Does that last question reek of essentialism? It should. On one level, of course, men and women *are* essentially different from one another. What we're talking about here, though, is not ordinary anatomical essentialism but cognitive essentialism—the discredited but suddenly strategically appealing idea that men and women register and process information in qualitatively distinct ways.

The Me Too movement, which rallied behind Kavanaugh's accusers, sits on an intellectual foundation of academic feminism, which has a strong cognitive-essentialist component. Note that I am distinguishing *academic* feminism, a relatively recent development, from original-recipe feminism. Through its first iterations, feminism stood in direct defiance of essentialism; it represented the antithesis of essentialist thinking. Against a prevailing wisdom that was not only ancient but seemed universal, feminists from Mary Wollstonecraft (1759–1797) to Betty Friedan (1921–2006) proposed that the intellectual, spiritual, and socioeconomic potentials of women should not be circumscribed or diminished by women's biological differences from men. Feminism therefore squared with, and derived its justifying arguments from, the ascendant values of the Enlightenment. These, again, are rational inquiry, socioreligious tolerance, and inalienable natural rights. Its progress is unthinkable absent those values.

Academic feminism, with its essentialist mindset, is one of many cartoonishly wrong turns feminism has taken in the last half century. Misanthropy. Misogamy. Self-help. Radical chic. Political correctness. Identity politics. Victimology. Recovered memory. Earth worship. Fetishization of the Other. Morally-blinkered fixation on abortion. The persistent, often comic devolution should not come as a surprise; the more successful a liberatory struggle is—and feminism has been both genuinely liberatory and extraordinarily successful—the less need there will be to sustain it. Thus, we find among contemporary feminists an increasingly desperate effort to discover and root out increasingly abstract vestiges of "patriarchy." As your boogeymen get smaller and smaller, your will to locate new ones begins to override your commitment to reason. And the only place you can shove aside reason in order to track down and curb stomp an infinitesimal is academia.

That is the case, as we have seen, with Critical Race Theory. It is also the case with academic feminism. Just as CRT provides two-bit race hustlers a pseudo-intellectual basis to dismiss empirical evidence and consistent logic in their real-world exertions, academic feminism provides Me Too hysterics a pseudo-intellectual basis to do the same. So, for example, in their popular feminist textbook *Introduction to Gender: Social Science Perspectives*, Jennifer Marchbank and Gayle Letherby write:

> Historically, the problem was not only that men were the primary focus of research but that the so-called "scientific" method was unquestioned as the best way to study both the natural and the social world. From this perspective, the view is that the "neutral knower" (the

> researcher) can be separated from what is known; that different researchers exposed to the same data can replicate results, and that it is possible to generalize from research to wider social and natural populations. In other words, the scientific method allows for the objective collection of facts by a value-neutral researcher: reality (the truth) is out there and the researcher can investigate and discover the "truth" independently of observer effects.[73]

If you remove the scare quotes, that's not a bad description of the axioms of scientific method. The analytical face-plant of the passage is that Marchbank and Letherby seem to believe that feminist insights of recent decades have somehow undermined those axioms—or, to use their preferred verb, "deconstructed" them. They've done no such thing, of course, nor *could they do such a thing*, except by deep-sixing the entire Enlightenment project and elevating subjectivity over objectivity, strong feelings over evidence and logic. Remember, yet again, that to deconstruct means nothing more than to futz around with secondary and tertiary senses of phrases and words in order to free associate your way to congenial banalities and non sequiturs. Scientific method cannot be "deconstructed"; its ontological validity is set before us every moment we are awake. If scientific method deserved those scare quotes, the building around you would be as likely to collapse a moment from now as remain upright. Or, to frame their position slightly differently, Marchbank and Letherby are arguing that it is an arbitrary expression of masculine hegemony, rather than an actual correspondence between concepts and reality, that keeps buildings from crumbling to dust. Marchbank and Letherby are living unironically in a classic Monty Python sketch in which El Mystico and Janet erect twenty-five story apartment high rises by hypnosis.[74] As long as the residents keep believing in the soundness of the structures, they will continue to stand.

Play out the logical consequences of the idea that knowledge derived by scientific method is no more or less valid, no more or less objectively true, than beliefs gleaned from personal experience. Every bigotry to which men have fallen prey, individually and collectively—including those bigotries that have historically stymied the human potentials of women—becomes justified.

Marchbank and Letherby seem utterly oblivious to those logical consequences:

> With all of this in mind, once we acknowledge the existence of several standpoints, it becomes impossible to talk about "independent truth" and "objectivity" as a means of establishing superior or "better knowledge" because there will always be alternative knowledge claims arising from contextually grounded knowledge of different standpoints.[75]

Impossible? Really? It's crucial to point out that the authors are not epistemological outliers. Far from it. The notion that independent truth and objectivity are considerations that can be cast aside when they conflict with subjective belief has become a truism of academic feminism. In a letter to the *New York Times Book Review* in July 1995, the renowned feminist critic Andrea Dworkin responded to the charge that her data on rape were exaggerated not by attempting to substantiate the numbers but by arguing that they were irrelevant to the truth value of her claims:

> I've been insulted a lot for my political views; but those views rest on women's experience, not social science studies (which often confirm my work). I believe that systematic violence is one way of keeping women second-class citizens. Nothing in my writing depends on statistics for either its truth or its effect.[76]

The position Marchbank and Letherby have staked out is therefore not a novel one. Their writings are, in a near-literal sense, textbook instances of academic feminism. Nor is academic feminism separable, as I compose these lines, from everyday feminism. You don't have to take my word for it. Here is Sian Ferguson, a contributing writer at the popular *Everyday Feminism* blog, on the subject of objectivity:

> Having your perspective dismissed because it isn't "objective" enough is an incredibly frustrating—and unfortunately common—experience. But a lot of us—both in social justice circles and out—tend to glorify objectivity in debates. Often, we think arguments and discussions are better when they're unemotional, unbiased, and unattached from personal perspectives—exactly as we were taught. By oppressive systems....In her book *Black Feminist Thought*, Patricia Hill Collins gives

> a brilliant explanation of how positivism—a school of thought that values objectivity and provable arguments—benefits white men the most. She also points out that black feminists and womanists have developed an alternative form of epistemology, or way of understanding knowledge, that she refers to as "black feminist thought." At risk of oversimplification, black feminist thought centers the lived experiences of marginalized people. It argues that subjectivity is valuable because people's lived experiences are valuable—because people's spoken truths are, in and of themselves, truths.[77]

It should go without saying, though I've said it again and again, that "people's spoken truths" are true only insofar as they correspond with a reality that exists independently of what they say. If they don't correspond with reality, "people's spoken truths" are just words that come out of their mouths; they have no inherent truth value and no particular claim on our attention except for what they may reveal about the shaky thought processes of people who believe that utterance equates with truth, that meaning is arbitrary, or that speech is equivalent to action. The world they imagine, the world they *desire*, is one bereft of if-then consequences.

Another epistemological swing-and-miss comes from Alex-Quan Pham, also from the *Everyday Feminism* blog:

> Not only is this urge to be rational holding us back, it unintentionally validates the logic of white supremacy as natural and positions the

> desire to fight oppression as excessive and outrageous.... The truth is, this constant emphasis on rationalism is a load of toxic garbage (and this is me being gentle with my words). It reeks of the rancid odor that develops when we squeeze our vast imaginations into tiny boxes labeled "pragmatic," "rational," and "reasonable." Being rational can often mean being willing to accept some aspects of oppression and watering down my politics.... In the context of anti-oppression work, limiting ourselves to rational thinking means that we're choosing to use the tools that make sense to our oppressors, which are usually tools made to hurt us. Rationalism means we're working within the framework of a system that was built to harm us in the first place.... We should be constantly interrogating why being rational has been presumed to hold inherent value, and we should be asking ourselves where we got that idea in the first place. The institutions that taught us what we know should be placed under suspicion.[78]

Again, there is nothing scandalous about the fact that nonsensical ideas trickle down from first-rate charlatans and wind up in the cognitive toolboxes of everyday mediocrities. There's a sucker born every minute and safe spaces on every college campus to which they can retreat when their opinions run into real-world headwinds. Once on campus, there are Stuart Smalley pep talks passing as academic disciplines, dispensing advanced degrees in nothing more than targeted ululation.

The *scandal* is that this sort of unrefined intellectual sewage has seeped through the campus floor and into the cultural groundwater, poisoning our collective understanding of the way things are.

The scandal, I repeat, is ours.

Test Cases

The fact that the Me Too movement rallied to the defense of Christine Blasey Ford in her false-to-near-arithmetical-certitude sexual assault allegations against Brett Kavanaugh does not discredit the cause around which the movement first coalesced. Nor does the fact that even now, unconscionably, Me Too activists have rarely backed off their support of Ford or of Kavanaugh's other accusers. Nor, in a wider sense, does the fact that those activists have adopted the feverish rhetoric and slapstick theorizing of academic feminism. It is necessary work to root out sexual abuse and harassment wherever they occur. That initial impulse was righteous.

The "Me Too" catchphrase dates back to 2006 and a series of Myspace posts by Tarana Burke, a social activist who had survived multiple instances of sexual assault as a teenager.[79] Her goal was to form a support network for others in her position and to call attention to the pervasiveness of women's sexual victimization by men. But the movement remained obscure for over a decade. It went viral, in the form of a hashtag, only after the *New Yorker* published firsthand accounts of brutal sexual misconduct by Hollywood producer Harvey Weinstein in 2017.

Weinstein's reckoning has come and gone, and he'll spend the rest of his life behind bars. It is crucial to recall, however, that prior to the *New Yorker* revelations, Weinstein's habits were an open secret in Hollywood. During the 85th Academy Awards telecast in 2013, host Seth MacFarlane joked that the nominees for Best Supporting Actress would "no longer have to pretend to be attracted to Harvey Weinstein."[80] MacFarlane's wisecrack came only a year after Meryl Streep affectionately called Weinstein "God" during her Best Actress acceptance speech at the Golden Globes,[81], and ten years after an auditorium of Hollywood notables, including Streep, director Martin Scorsese, actor Adrien Brody, and God himself (Weinstein) gave a long standing ovation to another film icon, Roman Polanski, when he was awarded a Best Director Oscar in absentia—despite the minor matter of his rape of a thirteen-year-old girl decades earlier.[82] How provincial of the rest of America, Hollywood seemed to say in unison, to hold "a personal mistake" (in actor Warren Beatty's memorable phrase) against an artist!

If the many anguished shouts of Me Too accomplished nothing except retroactively to shame the glittering hypocrites who winkingly hobnobbed with Weinstein and defiantly toasted Polanski, you'd have to say that they were the voices of angels. Public shaming, when it is directed at legitimately bad actors (in both the Hollywood and broader sense) is an honorable tradition.

People who do bad things should be made to feel badly about them.

That's true whether or not those bad things are criminal. Even if you are a fan of Louis C. K., for example, it is hard to criticize the public shaming of the comedian. He has, by his own admission, masturbated in front of younger female comedians, whose careers he was reasonably positioned to affect.

The mitigating circumstance offered by C. K. reads like a joke, though he seems to have meant it seriously: "At the time, I said to myself that what I did was okay because I never showed a woman my dick without asking first."[83] But since the incidents became public, C. K. has apparently discovered that what he did was wrong. "What I learned later in life, too late, is that when you have power over another person, asking them to look at your dick isn't a question. It's a predicament for them."

On the one hand, you'd think that asking a casual acquaintance to watch you masturbate would be intuitively recognizable as an imposition. You shouldn't need *The Idiot's Guide to Ethics* to arrive at that realization. I can recall vividly the time my dad taught me how to tie a necktie and the time my mom taught me to drive a stick shift. No one ever taught me not to masturbate in front of an audience, let alone a captive one, nor was that something I needed to be taught. The knowledge that public masturbation was wrong was part of the bundled software that came in the puberty package.

Me Too made the shaming of Louis C. K. not only possible but inevitable. Good for the activists. He deserved every iota of collective opprobrium that came his way. It is irrational, however, to gloss over the significant moral distinction between what C. K. did and what Weinstein did—though both clearly fall under the general category of "sexual misconduct" and are therefore properly targets of Me Too outrage. Weinstein sits in prison because he provably committed acts that meet statutory definitions of rape and sexual assault. C. K., by contrast, is not a criminal by any statutory definition, so if there is still a demand for his comic performances, as there seems to be, the free market should be both his judge and jury. We know who and what he is. The work of Me Too, in the matter of Louis C. K., should thus be finished.

Here is another way to draw the moral distinction. The identity of Weinstein's victims is ultimately irrelevant to his guilt. Due to his standing in the motion picture industry, he came into frequent contact with young actresses. But the acts that put him behind bars would have put him there if he'd done the same things to middle-aged housewives or superannuated women's studies professors. The contrast with Louis C. K. is, again, critical. If he'd invited comedy fans, rather than fellow comedians, to his dressing room for those special encores, informed them in advance of his intention to masturbate, and done nothing to prevent them from exiting, then what happened behind closed doors would have remained a private matter. It would still be icky. It would still be disheartening, perhaps even traumatizing, for the fans. But if the fans were of legal age and sober enough to form consent when they headed to C. K.'s dressing room, then their psychic injuries are their own responsibilities.

Which brings us to the peculiar case of the painter, photographer, and graphic artist Chuck Close (1940–2021). During the last decade of his life, two women, both younger artists, came forward with independent accusations of sexual harassment against Close. Their stories were essentially the same: Close had invited them to his studio, and, since they admired him, they had freely consented. Once in the studio, however, he'd asked them to take off their clothes—presumably, so that he could photograph them—and then, when they partly or fully complied, made lewd comments and asked to touch them. Both women refused, at which point Close attempted to pay them $200. One took the money; one didn't. Then, in both instances, the women left. A third woman also claimed Close had invited her to his studio and asked her to disrobe; when she refused, Close told her he was no longer interested, and she, too, left.[84]

The parallels to the case of Louis C. K. are obvious. But with two notable differences. None of the women complied with Close's most explicit requests, and Close was a paraplegic. Throughout the three encounters, Close remained bound to his wheelchair. He had no means to prevent the women from leaving his studio at any moment they desired, nor did he make the slightest effort to do so. After the women, inspired by the Me Too movement, went public with their complaints, Close himself apologized for his behavior. But his lawyer struck a more defiant tone:

> The bottom line of *all* the allegations is that no sexual act ever occurred—in fact, *Mr. Close never even touched any of your witnesses.* The most that can be said about the allegations against Mr. Close is that he uttered some words (some of which were sexually frank) which are alleged to have offended the sensibilities of these adult individuals.... This does not come close to reaching the level, and would only serve to cheapen the coin, of the terrible misconduct that rightly has been condemned of late.[85]

Close's sexual misconduct consisted of exploiting his celebrity in an awkward attempt to seduce young women, talking dirty to them, and then, after they had rejected his verbal advances, attempting to pay them as though they'd auditioned to be models. There was no physical menace, no overt or covert threat of retaliation, and nothing happened afterward to suggest a vendetta on Close's part.

If we suppose that full moral agency is the default condition of human adults, then it follows that what happened between Close and those three women is no one's concern but theirs.

The challenge for Me Too going forward is to figure out whether it wants to be a civil rights movement or a virtue crusade. Are Me Too goals narrow and pragmatic? Say, ending forced arbitration in workplace sexual harassment claims, thereby permitting victims to bring complaints directly to court?[86] Or are the goals more culturally momentous? Say, punishing sexual or even sexually suggestive conduct that doesn't end in mutual satisfaction on the basis of retroactive withdrawal of consent? If that second option seems outlandish, think of it not as a legal vanguard but as a cultural rearguard, an attempt to recapture the puritanical glories of Massachusetts Bay, except with the scarlet letter now pinned to tighty whities.

There is of course a third option, more cynical than the first two. Perhaps the correct way to regard Me Too is as politically weaponized subjectivity, a kind of emotional battering ram to be taken to policy disputes in support of feminist causes. The utility is obvious: *Don't you dare argue with me! This isn't a debate! I'm in pain! I'm a woman who's been victimized, so I'm going to speak my truth, and I don't have to explain myself to you or anyone else, and if you don't believe me, you're victimizing me again.*

Does that sound like a caricature? Consider the variation provided by Senator Mazie Hirono (D-HI) during the aforementioned Kavanaugh confirmation hearing: "I just want the men in this country to shut up and step up, and do the right thing for a change." When asked to expand on her point, Hirono told CNN:

> This kind of behavior, sexual harassment and sexual assault, has been going on...from time immemorial. It's not just something for the women in this country to care about; it's for all of us. That's why I've said to the men, "Just shut up and step up." And you know what? For the men who are offended by this, you should ask yourself, why are you offended by this? Why don't you ask yourself, what is there about this that offends you? We should all be holding together. We should all be treating each other like human beings. It's about time! It's not just for the women to bear this burden continuously. And guess what, the people who are perpetuating this kind of behavior, who are acting this way, are the men! That's why I said, "Face up! Step up!" [87]

There is, I re-reiterate, not a scrap of verifiable evidence that Christine Blasey Ford has ever *met* Brett Kavanaugh. Like Anita Hill before her, she is now a symbolic figure who serves to validate women's claims of victimization. The objective truth or falsehood of her accusations is beside the point.

The question at hand, however, is whether Hirono has encapsulated the essence of Me Too. If so, it's not an actual movement. It's a strategic non sequitur: when debating a political outcome favored by a majority of women, or even an especially vocal minority of women, collective injury trumps evidence and logic. The truth value of propositions is contingent on the victim status of the speaker. This is another form of essentialism. *My nature determines that my truth is truer than your truth. If you doubt what I'm telling you, under the circumstances, you are doubting the authenticity of my pain. More than that: you are doubting my very existence. You are erasing me.*

It's an effective non sequitur...if evidence and logic are not your friends.

Is there a reason to suspect that that's what Me Too is—a non sequitur?

The case of Avital Ronell suggests that there is indeed a reason.[88]

Ronell, a professor of German and comparative literature at New York University, described by a fellow NYU professor as "one of the very few philosopher-stars of this world," provably sexually harassed a graduate student, according to the findings of an eleven-month internal investigation. As a consequence, Ronell was suspended without pay for an academic year. But not fired. Nor were there loud protests, not when the charges first became public, not when the results of the investigation were announced, not even when Ronell resumed teaching the following year.

How can that be? Not a peep of protest, *in the age of Me Too*, at the return to classroom instruction of a sexual harasser? Not merely an *accused* sexual harasser, or a *credibly accused* sexual harasser, but a *proven* sexual harasser?

I don't think I'm going too far out on a limb to suggest that one factor is that Ronell is a woman, and the graduate student she sexually harassed is a man. The ironies whirling around the Ronell case are almost unbearable. At NYU, she holds the title of "Jacques Derrida Professor of Philosophy." She's a committed postmodernist, and on the way to her current eminence, studied under, was mentored by, and later co-taught with the great man himself. She describes herself, in Derridean-beyond-parody form, as "a thinker of the necessity of the unintelligible."[89]

She also, according to her victim, "kissed and touched him repeatedly, slept in his bed with him, required him to lie in her bed, held his hand, texted, emailed and called him constantly, and refused to work with him if he did not reciprocate."[90]

Still not enough irony for you?

The guy she harassed is gay. Ronell herself is a lesbian.

To be sure, the Ronell case *did* elicit a strongly worded response from prominent feminist academics across the world, though not quite the one you'd expect. Their letter is worth quoting at length:

> Although we have no access to the confidential dossier, we have all worked for many years in close proximity to Professor Ronell and accumulated collectively years of experience to support our view of her capacity as teacher and a scholar, but also as someone who has served as Chair of both the Departments of German and Comparative Literature at New York University. We have all seen her relationship with students, and some of us know the individual who has waged this malicious campaign against her. We wish to communicate first in the clearest terms our profound and enduring admiration for Professor Ronell whose mentorship of students has been no less than remarkable over

> many years. We deplore the damage that this legal proceeding causes her, and seek to register in clear terms our objection to any judgment against her. We hold that the allegations against her do not constitute actual evidence, but rather support the view that malicious intention has animated and sustained this legal nightmare.... We testify to the grace, the keen wit, and the intellectual commitment of Professor Ronell and ask that she be accorded the dignity rightly deserved by someone of her international standing and reputation. If she were to be terminated or relieved of her duties, the injustice would be widely recognized and opposed.[91]

The signatories to the letter comprise a who's who of post-modernist bluff-philosophy including Derrida's most famous translator Gayatri Spivak, she of such jewels of metaphysical insight as, "There is no harm in the will to knowledge, for the will to ignorance plays with it to constitute it—if we long to know we obviously long also to be duped, since knowledge is duping."[92]

The nonaggression pact between Professor Ronell and Me Too, therefore, raises a sticky question: Who's duping whom?

Being unintelligible, it would seem, means never having to say you're sorry.

Final Thoughts on Me Too

What lessons should we draw from these various cases: the Scottsboro Boys, Harvey Weinstein, Joe Biden, Brett Kavanaugh, Louis C. K., Chuck Close, and Avital Ronell? Believe the accuser, clearly. Unless the accuser is white and the accused black, in which case disbelieve the accuser and believe that the accused is a victim of systemic racism. Or unless the accuser is male and the accused female, in which case take into account the contributions that the accused has made to her field. But if the accuser is a white cisgendered woman, and the accused is a white cisgendered man, then believe the accuser. Unless the accused is a Democrat, running against a Republican. But if the accuser is a Democrat, and the accused is a Republican, and both are cisgendered and white, then believe the accuser, even in the total absence of verifiable evidence.

If *that's* the substance of Me Too, then it is indeed nothing more than a strategic non sequitur. It's a debate tactic, a rhetorical fallback when evidence and logic don't support the argument you're attempting to make. That's not to say that women aren't victimized by men, often horribly victimized, nor that their victimization does not stretch back to "time immemorial"—though of course the intellectual, spiritual, and socioeconomic prospects of women have improved drastically since the Enlightenment, and they would do well to compare and contrast their situations in pre- and post-Enlightenment societies. If inequities remain, and they do, the general trajectory of women's opportunities and outcomes in Western cultures is a good one. Things are moving in the right direction.

For that very reason, however, women have an abiding stake in the core values of the Enlightenment. Essentialism is inimical to those values. The bottom line is you either believe that women's brains and men's brains work the same way, that they are furnished with the same rational machinery, or you don't. If you *don't* believe it, then it is cruel to hold women to the strictures of rational argument, of logical examination and production of methodically gathered, verifiable evidence. If, however, you do believe that human beings, regardless of their sexual classification, are furnished with that same rational machinery, then you *must* hold women to those same strictures. But that means that the subjectivist thrust of the Me Too movement collapses.

CHAPTER FOUR

I Am He As You Are She

Getting Our Terms Straight

On November 15, 2021, the National Institute of Allergy and Infectious Diseases, led by Dr. Anthony Fauci, awarded a $205,000 grant to the Scripps Research Institute in Florida to pump male monkeys full of female hormones.[93] The goal of the study was to discover why HIV infections are now rampant among transgendered women.

Hmm. Let's see. You've got a virus that historically has disproportionately afflicted gay men, and now it is showing up disproportionately in transgendered women.

Yeah, it's a real puzzler.

This is what happens when you elevate subjectivity over objectivity, when you forget you're pretending, when you reject what's demonstrably true in favor of what a sympathetic group of people *wishes* were true. You start out with good intentions. But you end up flushing two hundred grand down the toilet and inspiring chimps to *feng shui* their cages.

It should go without saying, but I'll say it regardless, since in the current political climate *what should go without saying* needs to be said over and over: the reason HIV infections, previously found disproportionately in gay men, are now found disproportionately in transgendered women is that, despite what they believe themselves to be, despite their heartfelt demand that the rest of us agree with them, despite the willingness of the rest of us cater to that demand, *transgendered women are in fact men*. More to the point, with respect to the Scripps study, transgendered women are men who are engaging in the same set of behaviors by which the HIV virus has always been transmitted. You don't need a research grant to figure that out. You only need to acknowledge reality.

"Transgendered women" are men. "Transgendered men" are women.

That's the reality.

How do I, absent a medical degree, absent a psychologist license, and with not a piece of performance art to my credit, feel competent to render such a judgment? Because the debate isn't about medicine, psychology, or bullshit. It's about language. The words are not difficult: a man is an adult male human being; a woman is an adult female human being. That is what the words "man" and "woman" mean. So, too, "male" and female" have clear definitions. They are sexual classifications. They are not mysterious or conjectural. There are two and only two sexual classifications, and even in those vanishingly rare cases where observable anatomy is not immediately decisive, scientists can peer into a person's DNA profile and determine his or her biological sex with 100 percent accuracy.

These points become contentious only if you *deconstruct* the terms "man" and "woman," and "male," and "female," which is the reason gender studies is joined at the hip to postmodernism. By means of deconstruction—that is, targeted free-association, honey-glazed with pseudo-intellectual gibberish—you attempt to show how such terms are not the binaries that their dictionary definitions indicate, that they don't exhaust the categorical possibilities, and furthermore that they are not hard and fast designations but merely "assignments" that can be overridden at any point by imagination and will.

No one in their right mind honestly believes that.

Which is to say that many people *who are not in their right mind* honestly *do* believe it, and many others *who are in their right mind* dishonestly *say* they believe it. But how far through the looking glass are they willing to travel? According to the National Human Genome Research Institute:

> Identical twins (also called monozygotic twins) result from the fertilization of a single egg by a single sperm, with the fertilized egg then splitting into two. Identical twins share the same genomes and are always of the same sex. In contrast, fraternal (dizygotic) twins result from the fertilization of two separate eggs with two different sperm during the same pregnancy. They share half of their genomes, just like any other siblings. Fraternal twins may not be of the same sex or have similar appearances.[94]

If sexual classifications are assigned rather than observed, if they are fluid rather than fixed, then the National Human

Genome Research Institute is spreading misinformation. Identical twins are *not* always the same sex. Are you going to tell the folks in the lab coats, or should I?

How far through the looking glass are *you* willing to travel? Here is a self test, two propositions:

Proposition One: *"One characteristic common to all hominids is that only the female of the species can give birth."*

Proposition Two: *"Humans are unique among hominids in that both the female and the male of the species can give birth."*

Only one of those propositions can be true. Which is it?

It's possible, to be sure, that both propositions are false. It's possible that the reason primatologists tend to subscribe to Proposition One is that chimpanzees lack the cognitive and verbal capacities to communicate their true identities, that out in the savanna, when they let their hair down, male chimps are splatting out babies left and right, then suckling them in tender simian moments—right before those males gather in groups to tear off the penises of lone males (if indeed they are males) who trespass into their territory. Many textbooks, in that case, will have to be rewritten.

So, yes, it's *possible* that both propositions are false. But it's not possible, not *logically* possible, that both are true. Only one can be true. So what's your opinion? Are both false? Or is Proposition One true? Or Proposition Two? You've only got three possibilities. Before you answer, however, give a moment's thought to all those #IFuckingLoveScience memes you've posted to social media. Just how much do you fucking love science?

The answer is that Proposition One is true. Only female hominids give birth.

You know that, and I know that, and every primatologist on earth knows that.

Human beings are hominids. Therefore, only female human beings give birth.

So what does it tell you when mainstream media, including many traditional news sources, regularly report that men—male human beings—have given birth?

"Transgender man gives birth to a boy."[95]

"The dad who gave birth: 'Being pregnant doesn't change me being a trans man.'"[96]

"In a first for Illinois, transgender man who gave birth will be listed as the father on his baby's birth certificate."[97]

"Transgender man gives birth to healthy baby, talks navigating pregnancy as a man."[98]

"Trans man: 'How I coped with my shock pregnancy.'"[99]

"Transgender man gives birth after 'Grindr one-night stand' while transitioning."[100]

"Transgender man who gave birth to his son criticizes medical staff for calling him 'mother' and claims that it's 'important' to STOP automatically linking pregnancy with being a woman."[101]

Each of these headlines is howlingly false. Yet the reportage that follows each one is straightforward, without a hint of equivocation or irony. So let me re-reiterate, in case it still has not sunk in: a "transgendered man" is a woman. She is not a man *in a certain sense*; she is not a man *with an asterisk*. She is a woman, a female human being, to whom, by the rules of English grammar, female pronouns properly attach. If she is sincere in believing that she is a man, and there is no reason to suspect insincerity in any of the reported cases, then she is delusional.

According to Merriam-Webster, a *delusion* is "a persistent false psychotic belief regarding the self or persons or objects outside the self that is maintained despite indisputable evidence to the contrary." The fact that each of the women referenced in the headlines *gave birth to a living, breathing, human child* is indisputable evidence that she is female; the fact that each of them continues to insist that she is male is definitionally delusional.

Thus, a factual headline for each of these news reports would substitute the phrase "delusional woman" for "transgender man." But of course if you make that substitution, none of the reports is news. Delusional women have given birth, as Senator Hirono might say, since time immemorial.

"Transgender men" and "transgender women" are delusional women and delusional men. "Transgender children" are delusional children. They are to be pitied, not indulged, and their mental health needs addressed as compassionately as possible.

But what is the most compassionate way to address the mental health needs of a delusional person, male or female? That's a complex question. Surely, though, we can agree that acquiescing to his or her delusion isn't the way to go. You don't tell a schizophrenic man that the voices inside his head really and truly exist outside his head. You don't tell a woman suffering from multiple personality disorder that she really and truly is more than one person. That's not compassion.

Nor is it compassion to acquiesce to the delusions of a transgendered person. Nor is it progress, or justice in any sense of the word, to compel acquiescence on pain of ostracism or termination of employment.[102]

But wait! Haven't I overlooked the fact that *gender identity* and *sexual classification* aren't the same?

No, I haven't overlooked that. On the contrary, the reason the preceding analysis feels unsympathetic, and perhaps even cruel, is that I'm insisting that gender identity and sexual classification are not only different but remain distinct in our discussion. This runs counter to the shape-shifting rhetoric of transgender-activists who slide back and forth, sometimes conflating gender identity and sexual classification, sometimes separating them, in piecing together their arguments. If you keep them distinct, those arguments evaporate.

What is gender identity?

According to the World Health Organization, gender identity "refers to a person's deeply felt, internal and individual experience of gender, which may or may not correspond to the person's physiology or designated sex at birth."[103] The problem, of course, is that now you need to define gender, and here things start to get slippery, since the WHO's definition of gender rambles along for three digressive, decidedly Woke, and not altogether coherent paragraphs:

> Gender refers to the characteristics of women, men, girls and boys that are socially constructed. This includes norms, behaviors and roles associated with being a woman, man, girl or boy, as well as relationships with each other. As a social construct, gender varies from society to society and can change over time.
>
> Gender is hierarchical and produces inequalities that intersect with other social and economic

> inequalities. Gender-based discrimination intersects with other factors of discrimination, such as ethnicity, socioeconomic status, disability, age, geographic location, gender identity and sexual orientation, among others. This is referred to as intersectionality.
>
> Gender interacts with but is different from sex, which refers to the different biological and physiological characteristics of females, males and intersex persons, such as chromosomes, hormones and reproductive organs. Gender and sex are related to but different from gender identity....[104]

Integrating the WHO's definition of "gender" with its definition of "gender identity," we can thus say that gender identity refers to a person's embrace or rejection of the socially constructed behaviors and roles traditionally associated with being a woman, man, girl, or boy; these behaviors and roles may or may not match up with a person's sexual classification. When gender identity and sexual classification don't match, the person may or may not adopt the designation, "transgender."

None of that is especially problematic...as long as we keep gender identity and sexual classification separate in our minds. It only becomes problematic if we don't. Transgender-activists don't. They conflate gender identity and sexual classification. It is both a rhetorical tactic and an emotional sop.

That is the core of the debate over transgenderism.

The Meaning of "Is"

After his Senate confirmation as Assistant Secretary of Health and Human Services in October of 2021, Dr. Rachel Levine issued a statement expressing his heartfelt gratitude: "I am humbled to serve as the first female four-star officer of the US Public Health Service Commissioned Corps and first openly transgender four-star officer across any of the eight uniformed services."[105]

But, of course, he *isn't* the first female four-star officer of the US Public Health Service Commissioned Corps. He is another in a still-unbroken line of male officers to serve in that capacity, though he is apparently the first one *who identifies as female*. In the real world that exists beyond his self-perception, the world in which the rest of us are compelled to live, regardless of our willingness to embrace falsehoods in order to massage other people's feelings, Dr. Levine is a man who erroneously insists that he is a woman, serving in a position of great responsibility in the Biden administration.

It's an important job, and he has every reason to feel good about himself; it doesn't change who and what he is.

You'll search Dr. Levine's *Wikipedia* entry in vain to discover that he was born Richard Levine. By contrast with other biographical entries, the birth names of transgendered people are suppressed on Wikipedia following a July 2015 company edict: "It was decided that [the Wikipedia Style Manual] should be updated to say that a trans or non-binary person's former name should only be mentioned in the lead if they were notable under that name."[106]

Why are the birth names of transgendered or nonbinary people omitted on Wikipedia? Because the reportage or utterance of such information has been deemed taboo by transgender-activists. The taboo even has a name: *dead-naming.*

What clearer evidence could there be of the cluster of cultural neuroses that orbit the idea of transgenderism, or of our collective determination to indulge and infantilize those who identify as transgendered, than the existence of such a taboo? How can it be that transgendered people themselves fail to hear the condescension? *The sound of the name given to them when they were born is just too painful for their delicate psyches, so we must not communicate it in any way....*

I'm reminded of a Facebook exchange I had with an old graduate school friend several years ago. We were chatting about the cultural differences she'd experienced, as a lesbian, moving from New York City to the South. "My friend was assaulted because he used a men's room," she informed me. (Given the topic of this chapter, I imagine you can figure out what she meant.) Horrified, I told her that culture had nothing to do with a guy getting assaulted for using a men's room; I asked her if her friend had been robbed, or if he'd known his attacker, or if he had said or done anything that might have drawn his attacker's attention or in some way provoked him. During the entire exchange, all she could do by way of clarification was say, "You just don't get it," or, "You're still not getting it," or, "You're missing the point." Why? Because in order to accurately convey what had happened, she would have had to admit that her friend wasn't *really* a man, that she was a woman using a men's room, and that *that* was what had gotten the attention of her attacker.

Does that alter the morality of what happened in the restroom? No, if anything it makes what happened worse. (Call me old-fashioned, but I still cling to the idea that a man assaulting a woman is worse than a man assaulting another man.) The point here is that my friend and I went back and forth for five minutes before the truth at last dawned on me...and even then, even after the light bulb turned on, my friend couldn't bring herself to acknowledge the reality of the incident.

As I said earlier, the debate over transgender-recognition is ultimately a debate over language, about whether the meaning of words is stable enough to determine the truth value of propositions.

But back to Dr. (now Admiral) Levine. He is a man, according to the definition of "man" found in every English dictionary, who is from every indication sincerely convinced that he is a woman. He is wrong. He's not wrong to identify as a woman; he's not wrong to express that identification in the way he looks, the way he dresses, and the way he behaves. But as a factual matter, he is not a woman. The proposition "Rachel Levine is a woman" does not correspond with reality.

If you want to pretend that Rachel Levine is a woman, that's your affair. It's a private decision. But a society whose intellectual foundation is laid on the Enlightenment values of rational inquiry, socioreligious tolerance, and natural rights cannot impose a kindly fiction on its members, one by one or en masse.

This is not to say that transgenderism, the psychological condition, is not real. Recent studies have suggested that it may have a genetic component.[107] If the research pans out, then that would prove a measurable correlation between a transgendered person's genetic profile and his sense of distress at his sexual classification. But it still wouldn't prove that his sexual classification is erroneous.

Again, the comparison with schizophrenia is instructive. Schizophrenia also seems to have a genetic marker.[108] But that doesn't mean that the voices a schizophrenic hears inside his head exist outside his head.

Delusions are a reality. But the content of delusions is, by definition, unreal.

The point must be made over and over because the entire debate turns on it: gender identity is an altogether subjective phenomenon. It's a perception, often an unshakable perception, of who and what you are. Like all perceptions, however, it must be compared with reality to determine whether it is true or untrue—that is, whether or not it corresponds with reality. The fact that a perception is deeply felt, or even unshakable, does not count toward gauging that correspondence.

Like every other person to have served as assistant secretary of Health and Human Services, Dr. Rachel Levine is a man. He *feels* like a woman. He *identifies* as a woman. He *expresses* that identity in ways that are traditionally female. None of this is in dispute. None of it is problematic. Nevertheless, he *isn't* a woman. The meaning of "is" is distinct from the meaning of "feels"...or "identifies"...or "expresses." That which is, is. That which *could be*, *should be*, or in a perfect world *would be*, but isn't, is not.

The Nonbinary Bind

Oscar-nominated actress Elliot Page, formerly known as Ellen Page, teenaged star of the hit movie *Juno*, announced in late November 2020 that she was transgendered.[109]

> Hi friends, I want to share with you that I am trans, my pronouns are he/they and my name

> is Elliot.... I love that I am trans. And I love that I am queer. And the more I hold myself close and fully embrace who I am, the more I dream, the more my heart grows and the more I thrive. To all the trans people who deal with harassment, self-loathing, abuse, and the threat of violence every day: I see you, I love you, and I will do everything I can to change this world for the better.

Page subsequently clarified that she was neither male nor female but "nonbinary." That is, she does not identify as a man or a woman but as both, or neither—which hints at, but cannot fully account for, the reason she prefers the pronouns "he" and "they." That lacuna is filled, to a certain extent, by the term "queer," which means whatever people who identify as queer want it to mean; it is intended to be understood by non-queer people as roughly: "I don't fit into your traditional logical categories, so either love me for my irreducible singularity, or shut the fuck up."

Except, of course, that queer people, and nonbinary people, and people who mingle around the smorgasbord of initials, punctuation marks, and printer symbols being served at the end of "LGB," *do* in fact fit into traditional, logical categories. They may not want to fit into them, but the categories exist nevertheless, encompassing them, just as those categories have encompassed individual expressions of fauna ever since the earth started burping up sexually-bifurcated species all those eons ago.

More to the point, it is a philosophical error—specifically, Bishop Berkeley's error—to think that real things, such as the sexual bifurcation of species, cease to exist if we don't think about them. The tree that falls unobserved in the forest does indeed make a sound. Sexual bifurcation does indeed persist among hominids even if we choose to ignore it. The only thing new in the transgender debate is the rage-inspired, social media-driven demand of a mentally unbalanced cohort, as well as their cowardly enablers, that gender identity be substituted for sexual classification in formal and informal discourse.

Regardless of where you come down on the question, at least recognize what's going on: transgendered people claim the right to substitute their gender identity for their sexual classification. That claim is their sociopolitical alpha and omega, their will to power. Gender identity *must*, upon demand, override sexual classification. Subjective, unverifiable belief *must* override objective, verifiable reality.

That claim is not debatable, according to transgender-activists. To question it is an act of literal violence against the transgendered, an attempt to "erase" them, a denial of their very existence.[110]

But of course the claim *is* debatable, and we have been debating it here, rationally. Gender identity and sexual classification are, I repeat, different things. The former is mysterious and untestable, the latter empirical, and therefore they are by no means interchangeable. Acknowledging that reality denies the *existence* of no one; it merely holds that transgendered people are not what they believe themselves to be. Transgendered people are delusional people. Delusional people exist. They always have, and there is no reason to suspect they will cease to exist in the future. They deserve our sympathy and respect, and their natural rights are the same as everyone else's. But *no one*, including a transgendered person, has a natural right to force his delusions on others. You cannot compel others to disregard that which is observably true in favor of that which cannot be observed. You cannot compel them to play along, to act as characters in your fictional narrative, to pretend.

Notice, here, the difference from earlier civil rights movements. The cause of black liberation and women's liberation rested solely on that which was observable: the common humanity of the claimants. That is what made those earlier causes Enlightenment movements. By contrast, the cause of transgender rights cannot rest solely on the observable humanity of its claimants because the underlying argument depends on denying the observable. If transgendered people are *merely* human, their case is lost. Human beings are classifiable, without exception, into one of two biological sexes: male or female. Transgendered people are no less sexually classifiable than the rest of humankind. They do not control their sexual classification any more than they control any other element of their DNA profile.

This is yet another way of saying that not every human phenomenon is a social construct, as the postmodernists would have it. *Some* are, to be sure. Gender, insofar at it exists, insofar as it is more than a figment of our individual and collective imaginations, is indeed socially constructed—it is a deeply felt but empirically untestable mental state characterized by sensitivity to, and identification with, cultural stereotypes of masculinity or femininity. In the case of transgendered people, that sensitivity and identification come to eclipse their rational judgment of who they are. So, yes, gender is a social construct. Sex, however, is not. Sex is real. It exists independently of the thought processes of a thinker. It exists independently of our feelings about it. Sexual classification is binary and testable. In almost every case, it is testable by a cursory observation of anatomy. But sexual classification is testable in *every* case if you're willing to look hard enough.

Transgender-activists demand that transgendered people be treated not like everyone else but as special cases. Except they're *not* special cases, at least not with regard to their sexual classification. They are eccentric in how they live their lives. The sincerest among them are also, I repeat, delusional—a sad condition that correlates with a variety of poor mental health outcomes, including, in especially tragic instances, suicide.

But none of the above affects what transgendered people are *in reality*.

They are men or women, boys or girls. They can identify however they want. That's their natural right. They can present themselves in whatever ways make them happiest, in whatever ways they find intellectually and emotionally satisfying. That's also their natural right. But the reality is that they come with factory presets, and no regimen of plastic surgery, hormone treatment, and self-esteem massage is going to alter the brute fact of what they are.

Sexual classification is not something you get to decide, as desperately as you may wish it were. There is no natural right to overrule reality. You are what you are. Nothing more and nothing less.

None of this should be controversial. None of it is logically complicated, which again is the reason the transgender-recognition movement rejects the universality of basic logic and embraces postmodernist claptrap. It has to. Think about what happens if you begin to apply basic logic to the claims of transgendered people. Elliot Page was in a lesbian relationship when she announced that she was transgendered and nonbinary. She had a girlfriend. By definition, therefore, she and her girlfriend were either homosexual or bisexual prior to her announcement. What about after? If you take her announcement as determinative—in other words, if you substitute Elliot's gender identity for her sexual classification—then she and her girlfriend may or may not be bisexual, depending on how you interpret "nonbinary," but she and her girlfriend are no longer homosexual since she and her girlfriend are now sexually attracted to someone of a different sex. Homosexuals, by definition, are sexually attracted to the same sex.

(Notice, by the way, that at no point in the preceding paragraph did I use the pronoun "they," even though it would have made sense in at least three places. I couldn't use "they" because Elliot has claimed that as a singular pronoun. Humoring transgendered people with preferred pronouns is not a cost-free accommodation. It renders language less efficient. Language is like currency: as you debase it, it loses value and produces less meaning and more confusion.)

If Elliot Page is no longer classifiable as a woman, then *sexual orientation* must be tied to mental states rather than to anatomical preferences. It is, at least in a weak sense, elective. Your sexual orientation changes if you change your mind about who you really and truly are, or if your partner does...not by changing the fleshly object of your attraction but by changing your sexual classification. But what does that do to lesbian, gay, and bisexual identities? Their identity claims, after all, are far less epistemologically problematic, and far more empirically verifiable, than transgender claims. More to the point, LGB identity claims are also logically consistent.

The columnist and social critic Andrew Sullivan, himself a gay man, has wrestled with these (to be kind) paradoxes. It is worth quoting him at length:

> This is the deeply confusing and incoherent aspect of the entire debate. If you abandon biology in the matter of sex and gender altogether, you may help trans people live fuller, less conflicted lives; but you also undermine the very meaning of homosexuality. If you follow the current ideology of gender as entirely fluid, you actually subvert and undermine core arguments in defense of gay rights. "A gay man loves and desires other men, and a lesbian desires and loves other women," explains Sky Gilbert, a drag queen. "This defines the existential state of being gay. If there is no such thing as 'male' or 'female,' the entire self-definition of gay identity, which we have spent generations seeking to validate and protect from bigots, collapses." Contemporary transgender ideology is not a complement to gay rights; in some ways it is in active opposition to them.
>
> And the truth is that many lesbians and gay men are quite attached to the concept of sex as a natural, biological, material thing. Yes, we are very well aware that sex can be expressed in many different ways. A drag queen and a

rugby player are both biologically men, with different expressions of gender. Indeed, a drag queen can also be a rugby player and express his gender identity in a variety of ways, depending on time and place. But he is still a man. And gay men are defined by our attraction to our own biological sex. We are men and attracted to other men. If the concept of a man is deconstructed, so that someone without a penis is a man, then homosexuality itself is deconstructed. Transgender people pose no threat to us, and the vast majority of gay men and lesbians wholeheartedly support protections for transgender people. But transgenderist ideology—including postmodern conceptions of sex and gender—is indeed a threat to homosexuality, because it is a threat to biological sex as a concept.

And so it is not transphobic for a gay man not to be attracted to a trans man. It is close to definitional. The core of the traditional gay claim is that there is indeed a very big difference between male and female, that the difference matters, and without it, homosexuality would make no sense at all. If it's all a free and fluid nonbinary choice of gender and sexual partners, a choice to have sex exclusively with the same sex would not be an expression of our identity, but a form of sexist bigotry, would it not?[111]

Language matters. Logic matters. Language and logic are systems, to be sure, but they are ubiquitous, necessary systems. They are the givens of intellectual activity. You cannot step outside of them to critique them because the process of critiquing *anything* invokes them; whatever comes after, "Here are my reasons for skepticism about the uses of language and logic..." will be rooted in the effective use of language and logic. The process depends on their stability. They refer to real things and delineate real states of being. Yes, language and logic come with a degree of wiggle room. (*Deductive* logic, not so much, but *inductive* logic gets notoriously squishy the closer you look.) As a rule, however, the more malleable you suppose language and logic to be, the less functional they become.

Now, of course, the counterargument to the analysis I've just laid out is *shut the fuck up!*[112]

That was the trans-response to (formerly) beloved Harry Potter author J. K. Rowling in June 2020 when she took to Twitter to mock the ear-gagging circumlocution, "people who menstruate."

"'People who menstruate,' Rowling tweeted, "I'm sure there used to be a word for those people. Someone help me out. Wumben? Wimpund? Woomud?"[113]

This was enough to call down furies not only of the trans-community proper but of the trans-allied segment of the publishing world, typified by Gabrielle Bellot at Literary Hub:

> Time and time again, I've become accustomed to having to defend my womanhood when public figures declare that transgender women are not "real" women. Sometimes, I want to quietly sit back, avoiding the stress of having

> yet another prolonged argument with people who will call me "sir" at best and a rapist who should be euthanized at worst—for all trans women, the argument goes, are just men who want to sneak into women's locker rooms to do nefarious things.... At other times, I want to shout my barbaric yawp from the rooftops. I want to scream *no, fuck off, I won't let you demean me. This is who I am, this is foundational to my sense of self, and I didn't choose to be like this, would never pretend to be something that has brought me so much pain and loss.* I want to scream that I gave up so much when I came out as trans—my former home country, any hope of a good relationship with my family, old friends, any chance of a simple life—but stuck with it, anyway, because transitioning was essential for me, rather than some silly choice. I had to come out, or I couldn't keep living because the pain, the dissonant music of living a lie, was too much.... I want to yell in these moments, until I start to cry.[114]

The mixture of rage and pathos is the essence of the transgender case. It should sound familiar; it is the case of every baby who has been denied a pacifier. The fact we take that sort of rhetoric seriously is a reflection of our unwillingness to listen to the baby cry. Reality, however, is stubborn. Reality, as I said at the outset, doesn't give a rat's ass about you or me, or about how special we seem to one another, which means it also doesn't give a rat's ass if the baby cries the entire day. Transgendered women are *not* real women; insofar as language is capable of expressing truth, and logic capable of determining truth, transgendered women are *demonstrably* men who identify as women. They are real men who identify as women.

It's not as though Bellot himself hasn't been confronted with the truth. He has indeed looked the truth squarely in the face…and rejected it outright:

> To some, Rowling's tweets may seem anodyne. But if you read between the lines, their tone is patronizing, suggesting that trans people can wear whatever clothes we wish and use whatever language we like, but that in reality, we are living in a kind of silly delusion that people like Rowling merely politely tolerate.[115]

But that between-the-lines position is not patronizing. It is humane, charitable, and (not to be overlooked) *truthful.* What is untruthful is the claim that Bellot is a woman. Not only is that untruthful, it is unreasonable—as unreasonable, in its own way, as the bigoted belief that all transgendered women are interested in sneaking into women's locker rooms to do nefarious things. It is unreasonable to embrace provable falsehoods in order to spare people's feelings.

You can value people's feelings. You can value truth. Most of us value both. But sooner or later, inevitably, the two will clash. People's feelings *will* clash with the truth. That is the moment you'll have to declare your primary allegiance. Will it be to people's feelings? Or will it be to truth?

It is the question that lies at the heart of the Enlightenment confrontation with the Woke.

Swimming against the Current

On March 17, 2022, Lia Thomas of the University of Pennsylvania swam the 500-yard freestyle in Atlanta in slightly over four-and-a-half minutes. He finished comfortably ahead of Emma Weyant, a three-time national champion and Olympic silver medalist, to capture the Division I national collegiate women's championship in the event.

Thomas, in case you haven't heard, is a man who identifies as a woman.

At least one of Thomas's teammates at Penn was not thrilled at the development. "It's not necessarily an achievement in my mind," the teammate said, on condition of anonymity. "Women's records are separate from men's records. It's its own distinct category because no woman is going to be as fast as a man…we're just throwing away the definition of a record to fit into someone else's agenda of what it should mean to them when, in reality, it makes no scientific sense to do so."[116]

She's right, but with an *if.* It makes no sense, scientific or otherwise, for Thomas to compete against female swimmers…*if you believe that women's sports should exist in the first place.* Sports that require speed and strength are segregated into men's and women's competitions because men's physiology puts them at a significant advantage over women. Women compete against one another, but not against men. Serena Williams is a household name, and tennis fans' lives are richer for having watched her dominate the women's tour for two decades. But if she had been forced to play against male pros, we wouldn't know her name.

Lia Thomas, when he swam for the men's team at Penn during the 2018–19 season, was ranked 65th nationally in the

500-freestyle.[117] Now, competing as a woman against women, he's blowing away Olympic medalists.

None of which is to argue that male athletes who compete against female athletes are unbeatable. Thomas had in fact lost two months earlier in a shorter race to a Yale swimmer named Iszac Henig—who, ironically, was transitioning from female to faux-male; Henig had had her breasts surgically removed, but she had not yet undergone hormone replacement.[118] Even mixed martial artist Fallon Fox, after beating women opponents to bloody pulps in his first three fights, lost to a biological woman in his fourth.[119] Women who are at or near the pinnacle of their sports are sometimes able to hold their own against male also-rans or has-beens. Many of us recall that tennis legend Billie Jean King, in her prime, bested middle-aged Bobby Riggs in straight sets in the "Battle of the Sexes" at the height of the women's movement in September 1973. What's often conveniently forgotten is that earlier that year Riggs had clobbered the world's top-ranked female player, Margaret Smith Court, in straight sets 6-2 and 6-1.

The issue, in other words, is not whether biological men who compete against women will win every time. They won't, not if they were mediocre when competing against men, or if they are over-the-hill, or debilitated. But they will win a lot. Roughly ten thousand male sprinters—a number that includes runners who'll never catch a whiff of a world class men's race—have personal best times in the 100-meters faster than the current women's Olympic champion.[120] Worse still, the mere presence of men who identify as women in women's events will prevent an equal number of hopeful female athletes from achieving, or even glimpsing, their full athletic potential.

Australian handball player Hannah Mouncey, all six-foot-two and 220 pounds of him, toured on the Australian *men's* national team; after transitioning to faux-female, he claimed a slot on the *women's* national team...a slot that would otherwise have been filled by an actual woman.[121]

Think of the thousands of women's sports scholarships offered by colleges across the United States. Should those scholarships be open to men who are sincerely but delusionally convinced that they are women?

Which brings us to a final bitter irony.

Title IX is a 1972 civil rights law that forbids sexual discrimination by any school that takes money from the federal government. The wording of the statute is unambiguous: "No person in the United States shall, on the basis of sex, be excluded from participation in, be denied the benefits of, or be subjected to discrimination under any education program or activity receiving Federal financial assistance...."[122] But the Department of Education under President Obama interpreted the original language prohibiting discrimination based on *sex* to include discrimination based on *gender*—utilizing the now-familiar verbal bait-and-switch by which gender identity and sexual classification are conflated and substituted. That interpretation of the law was reversed under President Trump, then reinstated under President Biden. As of this writing, Title IX again prohibits discrimination based on gender identity...which means that a biologically male student who identifies as female is eligible to compete in women's and girls' sports.[123]

So you cannot discriminate on the basis of gender identity.

Setting aside the fact that biologically male students who believe themselves to be female are delusional, and biologically female students who believe themselves to be male are also delusional, and thus that the Obama-Biden interpretation of Title IX in effect codifies delusion as reality, the rule that you cannot discriminate on the basis of gender identity is also logically anarchic. If you enforce it consistently, you undercut not only the original intent of the law but also the (presumptive) goal of making women's sports more inclusive.

Reason it out.

Lia Thomas is now the reigning national women's champion in the 500-freestyle. He surely wouldn't be the 500-freestyle champion if he were racing against male swimmers; we know that since he was never ranked higher than 65th nationally when he *was* racing against male swimmers. Suppose that the national men's champion in the 500-freestyle decides to consolidate the two titles, men's and women's. Or that the second-place finisher decides he'd like a crack at the women's title...or that the third-place finisher decides he would. Who'll tell them that they're not eligible to compete? The National Collegiate Athletic Association? What would that argument sound like?

"Sorry, you can't compete against women because you're not transgendered?"

Except that means you're discriminating against them *on the basis of gender identity.*

Let's run through that one more time: If transgendered Lia Thomas is allowed to compete against women, but the cisgendered men's champion is not allowed to compete against women, then by definition the cisgendered men's champion is being discriminated against on the basis of his gender.

That's a violation of the Obama-Biden interpretation of Title IX.

Maybe the scenario of a top-ranked cisgendered male swimmer deciding to compete against female swimmers seems far-fetched. If so, consider those ten thousand male sprinters who are faster than the current women's 100-meter Olympic champion. Think about number 9,999: cisgendered, sporting a blue vest with a yellow logo, stocking shelves at his local Walmart. Think he might be tempted to go for the gold, with a fortune in free publicity, positive and negative, awaiting him?

The Emperor's New Culture

The prospect of cisgendered male athletes dominating, and ultimately obliterating, women's sports follows logically from the desire to conflate sexual classification with gender identity under Title IX guidelines. It would be a knockdown argument against that reading of Title IX…if not for the postmodern rejection of logical consistency that runs through Woke thought. Whatever line of argument gets you where you want to go, that's the line you take—even if that argument is not a line but a squiggly mishmash, even if you have to stamp your feet to extinguish the glow of a smoldering *if-then*, even if your final position rests on nothing more substantial than, *don't go there, girlfriend!* Say what you need to say, as loudly and proudly as you need to say it. You're a victim, so the Great American They are supposed to listen to you.

Logic be damned.

Here is an if-then to consider: If a biological male becomes female by the sincere belief that he is female, then why doesn't a white woman become black by the sincere belief that she is black? The question arose in 2015 in the person of Rachel Dolezal, president of the Spokane, Washington, chapter of the National Association for the Advancement of Colored People, who had claimed to be mixed-race, and, like many mixed-race people, had lived her adult life as if she were black, but whose entire lineage, it turned out, traced to Northern and Central Europe—and whose childhood photos resemble Greta Thunberg, with traces of Pippi Longstocking.[124]

Rachel Dolezal, however, *identified* as black.

Her claim of transracialism was immediately and universally denounced by the very same Woke voices who insist that claims of transgenderism cannot be doubted. Not only was Dolezal's claim denounced, it was mocked. She became a punchline on late night television.

But how can transracialism be dismissed out of hand if transgenderism is indubitable? Why is Rachel Dolezal a laughingstock but Rachel Levine a trailblazer? Is the argument that sexual categories are fluid, but racial categories are hard and fast? You may have a difficult time convincing professional anthropologists to sign off on that one, since both the American Anthropological Association[125] and American Association of Biological Anthropologists[126] agree that "races" are artificial constructs.

Nevertheless, according to feminist philosophers Robin Dembroff and Dee Payton, there *is* a reason to embrace transgenderism and reject transracialism:

> When considering whether to revise rules for gender or race classification, we think that there are important considerations at both

> the population level and the individual level. While it is important and good to value a person's autonomy and respect their identifications, we also think this good must be weighed against the population-level effects of revising our classifications. In cases where revising a classification would have a negative sociopolitical impact that outweighs the good of respecting how an individual identifies, we think that the classification should not be revised. And we think that revising the rules of race classification to accommodate transracial identification into Blackness is a case like this.[127]

Notice that Dembroff and Payton's argument is decidedly Woke and purely pragmatic. It doesn't address the truth value of claims of transracialism versus claims of transgenderism but the moral consequences of accepting one versus the other. Correspondence with reality is irrelevant. To Dembroff and Payton, this is strictly a should-we/shouldn't-we question. Revising race classifications "would have a negative sociopolitical impact that outweighs the good of respecting how an individual identifies"; therefore, they're *agin it.*

Luckily, revising sexual classifications carries no potential for negative sociopolitical outcomes....

How do you respond to such arguments?

One time-tested option is to laugh at them.

That is the approach taken by the satirical website, the *Babylon Bee*. But on March 20, 2022, the *Bee* had its Twitter account briefly suspended for violating Twitter's rules against "hateful conduct." The explanation from Twitter read, "You may not promote violence against, threaten, or harass other people on the basis of race, ethnicity, national origin, sexual orientation, gender, gender identity, religious affiliation, age, disability, or serious disease."[128]

What was the nature of the *Bee*'s hateful conduct?

It had named Rachel Levine its "Man of the Year."

Twitter is a private company and can establish and enforce its own rules for the use of its services. But a number of relevant facts should be noted:

Levine is a high-ranking, high-profile, government official and, by any reasonable measure, a public person. He is also a man who falsely claims to be a woman.

The *Bee*'s "hateful" tweet came a week after *USA Today* honored Levine as one of its women of the year. The joke thus clearly targeted *USA Today* as much as it targeted Levine.

More to the point, the plain sense of the joke doesn't promote violence against, threaten, or harass anyone; it does nothing of the sort, unless you're willing to *deconstruct* the meaning of violence, threats, and harassment into concepts so vague and unrecognizable that even an eye roll qualifies as an attack.

Nevertheless, Twitter suspended the account of the *Babylon Bee.*

How worried should the rest of us be?

Very worried. Yes, Twitter is a private company. But that means it's responding not to voters—which would be the case if a government entity had punished the *Bee*—but to cultural trends. Voters are volatile. They are swayed by current events and by the passions engendered in the knockabout of a weekly news cycle. Culture, on the other hand, is phlegmatic. It oozes in a particular direction and is very difficult to get moving in reverse.

Culture, when it is a healthy culture, gradually aligns itself with what is demonstrably true. That's virtually a tautology because the intellectual and emotional heft of culture is weaker than the intellectual and emotional heft of reality. If culture becomes antagonistic to what is demonstrably true, if what is demonstrably true becomes what is culturally hateful, then a crack-up is coming—and it's not going to be reality that cracks.

The surest sign of a decadent culture isn't its readiness to license varieties of personal abuse and degradation, or even its elevation of immediate pleasure over long-term sobriety. The surest sign of cultural decadence is a readiness to reject as hateful what is demonstrably true.

CONCLUSION

The Looming Disintegration

Much of the debate over Wokeness, as I've endeavored to show, is actually a debate over whether truth—that is, a correspondence between what's thought and said and a reality that exists independently—can be had. That sort of truth depends on the capacity of language to refer unambiguously to real things and on the power of logic to narrow down and identify correspondences. These are philosophical issues. If you are determined to ignore the referential quality of words as well as the methodologies of deductive and inductive logic, then you can spout any nonsense you want, at least until a louder voice comes along to drown you out. Do not underestimate the political implications of that last point. Voices conflict, individually and collectively. You either hash out your conflicts by attempting to determine what is objectively true, or you simply yell louder. The arena is either intellect or will. And if it's will, then truth has no advantage over nonsense.

The fact that the Woke are currently the loudest voices in academia is an unfortunate, but not an unpredictable, development. Because of its insular nature, the university is always susceptible to bad ideas; this is a special danger in the humanities and social sciences, where reality checks are often optional and occasionally nonexistent. Only in such an environment would you get the necessary confluence of vacuous speculation, interdisciplinary feedback loops, and hierarchies of institutionalized cowardice for a phenomenon such as Wokeness to take root.

Now that is has taken root, the question becomes whether, and by what means, it can be uprooted. If logic is off the table, because it is allegedly an instrument of oppression, and empirical evidence is off the table, because "reality" is a social construct, what remains? It is easy enough to ridicule the student-automatons at Middlebury College who shut down a guest lecture by the political scientist Charles Murray by rising as one to recite, "Science has always been used to legitimize racism, sexism, classism, transphobia, ableism, and homophobia, all veiled as rational and fact, and supported by the government and state. In this world today, there is little that is true 'fact.'"[129] But what happens when the ridicule falls on deaf ears? If you've read this far, you likely understand how illiberal, how bourgeois, and how ultimately preposterous those Middlebury students are. But they can't hear you laughing at them. What they hear, instead, is a sympathetic professoriate and a supine administration applauding their courage.

The first observation to make about those Middlebury protesters and their preening, self-righteous peers at dozens of other colleges across the United States is that they're done. Not done in the sense of having accomplished a task, but done in a far more ordinary and digestible sense: they're fully cooked and ready to be consumed; premade earthworm meals; ragged claws scuttling through the halls of ivory towers.

I don't intend that judgment to be cruel. I take no pleasure in mentioning it. But ask yourself this: In the last several millennia of recorded human endeavor, can you name one writer, one artist, one thinker, one remotely interesting, original, or memorable person who, as a young adult, wanted to know *less* about the world? Don't misunderstand me. Those students may eventually recognize the utility of manners; they may grow up to be pillars of their communities, loyal friends, and loving parents. Intellectually, however, people who attempt to shut down ideas have thrown in their lot with fanaticism. They may not be as bug-eyed as demon-hunters of the past—though many have given it the old college try and tellingly have acquired faculty apologists—but they are one in spirit.[130] They have taken a stand not merely against a particular idea but against civilization itself, whose lifeblood is the interplay of ideas. Like fanatics in every age, they come and go with the tide. They are born. They gesture and copulate. They grow old and die. Their ingredients pass back into the earth, and they are forgotten. That's it. That's the entire ride. Here one moment, gone the next.

The second observation to make is that, in theory, the problem of student protesters shutting down speech has a very straightforward solution; it is perhaps the easiest problem to solve in American public life: expel them. Every last one of them. Let them get on with their fanatical little lives sooner rather than later. It is, so to speak, a no-brainer. They post videos on social media. *They record themselves shutting down speech.* Thus, they record themselves violating not only the right of an invited speaker to express his ideas but also the right of their fellow students to hear that speaker's ideas.

The fact that there have been no mass expulsions must therefore be seen as a signal. It is a signal that feelings have overtaken reason, that fanaticism is regnant, that the will to defend the expression of ideas—for the specific purpose of gauging their truth value—has been eclipsed on American college campuses.

That, in turn, suggests that our current system of higher education, *as a system of higher education*, is no longer viable. The humanities and social sciences are undergoing a reversion to an earlier model of pedagogy. Prior to the Enlightenment, most universities were sites of religious instruction. They trained clergy. Harvard was founded in 1636, a mere six years after the settlement of Massachusetts Bay, to ensure that future generations of New England Puritans would be served by learned ministers. That purpose is found among Harvard's original "Rules and Precepts":

> Let every student be plainly instructed, and earnestly pressed to consider well, the main end of his life and studies is, to know God and Jesus Christ which is eternal life and therefore to lay Christ in the bottom *[i.e., at the base of the boat, to keep it steady in the water]*, as the only foundation of all sound knowledge and learning. And seeing the Lord only giveth wisdom, let everyone seriously set himself by prayer in secret to seek it of him.[131]

Once you realize that Wokeism is a religion, you begin to understand that instruction in Woke curricula at the university level is baptism by accreditation. It's witness and testing. You gather for three hours a week to dwell in the spirit, dedicate yourself to individual rituals and collective causes, despair the fallen state of humanity, call out and cast out devils, read sacred texts and memorize venerable chants, then venture out to spread the gospel. The end is performative, sacramental. *Let me tell you the many ways you are oppressed so that you may be a river to the unwashed masses.*

That is the current state of the humanities and social sciences.

It is a long-term civilizational disaster, but it is also a short-term viability crisis for higher education because instruction in the STEM fields at American universities remains traditional, focused, and globally competitive. The reversion of the humanities and social sciences in America to religious preparation cannot coexist with the ongoing excellence of STEM instruction. Something has to give. If history textbooks must be revised as a sop to self-esteem, why not biology textbooks? Pity the poor seahorse, hitherto famous as the only species in which the male gives birth. But for how long? You cannot be taught in your morning sociology seminar that the pursuit of objectivity is an instrument of white supremacist culture, which must therefore be deconstructed, and then accept that in your afternoon calculus class the square root of 169 is *objectively* 13.

Mustn't we interrogate the definitions of "square root," "13," and "169" in order to lay bare their internal contradictions? Don't we have to inquire how the insistence that there is one, and only one, correct square root of 169 serves to perpetuate many of the injustices of the status quo?

"Is $E=mc^2$ a sexed equation? Perhaps it is...."

Confronted by two irreconcilable visions of the universe—one in which reality is a social construct endlessly negotiated among discourse communities; one in which reality is a given to which we adjust our thoughts and statements—students are voting with their feet. Nationwide, the number of humanities and social science majors is mostly dropping, and the number of STEM majors is mostly rising.[132] One disturbing exception to that trend, however, is a 5 percent uptick in cultural, ethnic, and gender studies majors between 2011 and 2017—which proves, I suppose, that the varieties of religious experience keep multiplying, and that many students would rather hug it out than engage in the intellectual heavy-lifting required to discover objective truth…though perhaps the growth in these majors is also testament to the burgeoning field of diversity, equity, and inclusion jobs in education, business, and government. (Whether anyone whose job title includes the word "diversity," "equity," or "inclusion" *has* an actual job is a topic for another book.)

Regardless, a disintegration is on the horizon.

It is natural to think that the demand for severing ties will come from the professoriate on the STEM side, from a desire not to sully their professional reputations by sharing university affiliations with the *Wokeanschauung* described in this book. More likely, though, the demand will come from the humanities and social science side, from the unbearable adjacency of reality-based standards and scholarship to their mystical, communal fiefdoms. Entrance into STEM fields requires rigorous, objective standards of assessment, as does progress in them and graduation from them. Rigorous, objective standards of assessment, however, don't produce equity. They don't produce diverse student populations. Asian students are currently overrepresented in STEM, black students underrepresented; [133] male students are overrepresented, female students underrepresented.[134] According to the tenets of Wokeism, demographic imbalances of that nature constitute de facto proof of racial and gender bias since in an unbiased system every demographic would be equally represented. How long will student-activists, encouraged by humanities and social science faculty, tolerate such rank injustice on their campus? How long until the automatons invade STEM classrooms? *Hey, hey, ho, ho! Standard testing's got to go!*

I reiterate: something has to give.

Whichever side precipitates the disintegration, it will be a necessary development. Higher education is a serious intellectual endeavor, and nothing is less intellectually serious in contemporary public life than Wokeism. Empirical observation, mathematical inquiry, deductive reasoning, and falsifiability are the sine qua nons of higher education. As courses of study in the humanities and social sciences depart from such things, they cease to be higher education in the post-Enlightenment sense.

Suppose, therefore, that STEM disciplines go their own way—either by their own choice or because they are driven off by the demand to diversify their curricula, faculty, and student population. The disciplines themselves, in that case, will not cease to exist; there will still be a demand for instruction in them, so they will be compelled to reform as STEM-signature universities. The mission statements of these universities will necessarily commit them to empirical observation, mathematical inquiry, deductive reasoning, and falsifiability—which means that they will be the least Woke places on earth.

No such school exists at the moment. There isn't even a model for one yet. (Even Massachusetts Institute of Technology, which you would think might be immune, offers its students a rich buffet of empty intellectual calories in race and gender studies.) The question then becomes whether a true STEM-signature university will even bother to house curricula in the humanities and social sciences. If they do, then those curricula will also necessarily be centered on the sine qua nons mentioned above.

There is indeed a strong case, a *humane* case, for rounding out STEM education with what nineteenth century critic Matthew Arnold famously called, "the best that has been thought and said," even if the faces behind those thoughts and sayings don't form a gorgeous mosaic. Combine the subject matters of the humanities and social sciences with something like the methodological rigor of STEM, and before long you'll have cohorts of classically educated young Americans willing to stand athwart the cultural decline, willing to stem our devolution into a gelatinous mass of magical thinking, self-pity, and infantile rage.

If it seems, in these concluding remarks, that I'm too focused on the future of higher education, or that I'm attaching outsized weight to the capers of campus clowns, consider that the elevation of subjectivity in CRT, Me Too, and transgender-recognition was strictly an academic curiosity before it jumped the shark and landed in your kid's sixth grade homework assignment, your company's required sensitivity training, and your city council's decision not to prosecute shoplifting. The postmodern, anti-realist movements in the humanities and social sciences were running jokes among traditional scholars in all fields—right up until they weren't. Right up until free-association became a standard investigative methodology, stamping your feet became a familiar form of argument, and literal nonsense became conventional wisdom. Let me quote again Derrida's translator, Gayatri Spivak: "There is no harm in the will to knowledge, for the will to ignorance plays with it to constitute it—if we long to know we obviously long also to be duped, since knowledge is duping."[135]

Duping...bluffing. Po-tay-to...*différance.*

Welcome to the humanities and social sciences, circa 2022.

It happened. It's accomplished. That genie ain't going back in the bottle. There is no logical, evidence-based argument to coax it back because the Woke have been awakened to the evils of logical, evidence-based arguments. Their self-perception is transcendent. They see their teleology as liberatory rather than totalitarian; they want to remake the world into a "safe space." Safe from what? *Safe from evidence and logic.* Safe from empirical observation and analysis. Safe from dispassionate inquiry. Safe from deductive reasoning. Safe from falsifiability. These are the things that hem in the Woke, that prevent them from feeling what they want to feel, that leaden their imaginations.

The Woke, therefore, seek not only to consolidate their hegemony on American campuses but to project that hegemony beyond humanities and social science classrooms, to reconceive reality in their image. But, as I've labored to show, reality doesn't bend to our conceptions. Civilizations do; they collapse under them. But reality doesn't. Reality endures. History isn't altered by our feelings about what happened. Women's recollections of trauma are no more or less reliable than men's. Human beings, in every case, are sexually classifiable as either male or female, and their acceptance or rejection of their classification doesn't affect their classification. That's reality. Even ethnic and gender studies professors are ultimately answerable to reality. They've just landed gigs where they get to pretend otherwise.

But reality knocks at all of our doors, regardless of our ideologies. You can bury your head under the covers; reality will slide in next to you, and it will whisper into your ear, in a persistent, resonant voice, that you are full of crap. There is no safe space to escape it. Remember that the purpose of a safe space is not to protect people; it's to protect people's feelings, to set their feelings beyond rational debate. To render them true by virtue of their being sincerely felt.

Safe spaces are unreal spaces. Which means safe spaces don't exist. Not even, truth be told, on campus. The only support a campus can provide, in the struggle to spare your feelings, is a superstructure of pretense, a distribution mechanism of cotton balls to stuff into your ears. Sooner or later, however, reality *will* intrude.

That's the truth.

Yes, in the gospel sense, if you go in for that sort of thing, the truth sets you free. But in the common sense, the truth does nothing of the sort. On the contrary, it binds you, it humbles you, it challenges you to become more reasonable. How you react to the truth, of course, is a matter of conscience. You can ignore it and hope that no one notices, or you can adjust to it. But if, for the sake of people's feelings, you can be made to admit, or even worse to believe, that what's true is false, or what's false is true, then you're lost. Intellectually and morally, you're lost.

ENDNOTES

1 Friedrich Nietzsche, *The Antichrist,* Section 46, final paragraph

2 Philip K. Dick, "I Hope I Shall Arrive Soon," first published as "Frozen Journey" in *Playboy,* December 1980

3 John Lennon, "Ballad of John and Yoko," 1969

4 James Randerson, "What DNA Can Tell Us," *The Guardian*, April 26, 2008, https://www.theguardian.com/science/2008/apr/27/genetics.cancer#:~:text=The%20simplest%20thing%20DNA%20can,(which%20makes%20them%20female)

5 Rene Descartes, *Meditations on First Philosophy*, 5:46–47

6 *Ibid*

7 George Berkeley, "A Treatise Concerning the Principles of Human Knowledge," in *The Works of George Berkeley, Bishop of Cloyne* (London: Thomas Nelson, 1949), Volume II, 42

8 *Ibid*

9 Immanuel Kant, *Critique of Pure Reason*, § VI

10 Jacques Derrida, *Of Grammatology* (Baltimore: Johns Hopkins University Press, 1974), 61

11 *Ibid.*, 65

12 Jacques Derrida, *Dissémination* (Chicago: University of Chicago Press, 1981), 207

13 Roland Barthes, *The Pleasure of the Text* (New York: Noonday Press @ Farrar Straus and Giroux, 1975), 3

14 Michel Foucault, *Language, Counter-Memory, Practice: Selected Essays and Interviews* (Ithaca: Cornell University Press, 1977), 181

15 *Ibid.*, 185

16 The fact that postmodern scholarship and parodies of postmodern scholarship are hard to tell apart is shown by the fact that actual parodies keep being accepted in peer-reviewed journals. See, for example, the "Sokal Hoax" of 1996 and "Sokal Squared" of 2017

17 Luce Irigaray, "*Sujet de la science, sujet sexué?*" from *Sens et place des connaissances dans la société* (Paris: Centre National de Recherche Scientifique, 1987), 95–121

18 Gayatri Spivak, translator's preface to *Of Grammatology*, by Jacques Derrida (Baltimore: Johns Hopkins University Press, 1974), *lxxvi*

19 Barbara Johnson, cited by John M. Ellis in *Against Deconstruction* (New Jersey: Princeton University Press, 1989), 6

20 "A Black Feminist Critique of Antidiscrimination Law and Politics," in *The Politics of Law: A Progressive Critique*, ed. D. Kairys (New York: Pantheon, 1990), 195–218

21 Cited by columnist Melissa Chen in a discussion with author Steven Pinker at a talk hosted by the Foundation Against Intolerance and Racism (FAIR) on November 19, 2021, "On being rational, with Steven Pinker and Melissa Chen," https://fairforall.substack.com/p/on-being-rational-with-steven-pinker

22 Ibram X. Kendi, *How to be an Anti-Racist* (New York: Penguin-Random House, 2019), 17–18

23 For a brief account of the role of black advocacy in crack cocaine sentencing guidelines, see Arun Venugopal, "Black Leaders Once Championed the Strict Drug Laws They Now

Seek to Dismantle," at WNYC News, August 15, 2013, https://www.wnyc.org/story/312823-black-leaders-once-championed-strict-drug-laws-they-now-seek-dismantle/

24 "Read Ibram X. Kendi's Testimony in Support of the Working Group Recommendation to #SuspendTheTest," Boston Coalition for Education Equity, October 21, 2020, https://www.bosedequity.org/blog/read-ibram-x-kendis-testimony-in-support-of-the-working-group-recommendation-to-suspendthetest

25 Joshua Goodman and Melanie Rucinski, "Increasing Diversity in Boston's Exam Schools," Harvard Kennedy School, October 2018, https://scholar.harvard.edu/files/joshuagoodman/files/rappaport_brief.pdf

26 A 2008–2009 NYC study found that 77 percent of Asian students were eligible for free lunches, compared with 90 percent of Hispanic students and 85 percent of black students; white students checked in at 48 percent, https://www.the74million.org/article/new-study-of-70000-nyc-kids-shows-achievement-gaps-widening-over-time-except-for-asian-students/

27 See Twitter thread: SF Guardians (@sfguardians), "30 Reasons to Recall the SF School Board," March 18, 2021, https://twitter.com/recallsfboe/status/1372753629573128206/photo/1

28 KQED New Staff, "Censured SF School Board Member Alison Collins Sues District, Colleagues for Constitutional Rights Violations," April 1, 2021, https://www.kqed.org/news/11867599/censured-sf-school-board-member-alison-collins-sues-district-colleagues-for-constitutional-rights-violations

29 Chart reproduced at The Bulwark: Robert Tracinski, "Where Progressives and the Alt-Right Meet," July 21, 2020, https://www.thebulwark.com/where-progressives-and-the-alt-right-meet/

30 See video: Black on Black Education, "The Science of Black Teaching (featuring Maria Akinyele)," YouTube, April 28, 2021, https://www.youtube.com/watch?v=eWOuZFxAlwA&t=2s

31 See "EdFix Episode 23: Fighting Racism With Mathematics," George Washington University, the Graduate School of Educational and Human Development, https://gsehd.gwu.edu/edfix-episode-23-fighting-racism-mathematics

32 *Ibid*

33 "K-12 Math Ethnic Studies Framework (20.08.2019)," Seattle Public Schools, https://www.k12.wa.us/sites/default/files/public/socialstudies/pubdocs/Math%20SDS%20ES%20Framework.pdf

34 *Ibid*

35 *Ibid*

36 *A Pathway to Equitable Math Instruction: Dismantling Racism in Mathematics Instruction,* https://equitablemath.org/wp-content/uploads/sites/2/2020/11/1_STRIDE1.pdf

37 *Ibid*

38 University of Illinois Professor Rochelle Gutierrez: "On many levels, mathematics itself operates as whiteness. Who gets credit for doing and developing mathematics, who is capable in mathematics, and who is seen as part of the mathematical community is generally viewed as white." (From Gutierrez's essay, "Political *Conocimiento* for Teaching Mathematics: Why Teachers Need It and How to Develop It.") Gutiérrez also states that all knowledge is "relational" and that "things cannot be known objectively; they must be known subjectively."

39 Purdue University Professor and head of its School of Engineering Education Donna Riley: "Rigor accomplishes dirty deeds, however, serving three primary ends across engineering, engineering education, and engineering education research: disciplining, demarcating boundaries, and demonstrating white male heterosexual privilege. Understanding how rigor

reproduces inequality, we cannot reinvent it but rather must relinquish it, looking to alternative conceptualizations for evaluating knowledge, welcoming diverse ways of knowing, doing, and being, and moving from compliance to engagement, from rigor to vigor." Donna Riley, "Rigor/Us: Building Boundaries and Disciplining Diversity with Standards of Merit," *Engineering Studies* 9, no. 3 (2017), https://www.tandfonline.com/doi/full/10.1080/19378629.2017.1408631

40 Aysa Gray, "The Bias of 'Professionalism' Standards," *Stanford Social Innovation Review,* June 4, 2019. "How people manage their time in relationship to work plays a huge role in their success. Research from a 2017 Career Builder survey in the United States, for example, found that 41 percent of all employees are terminated due to continual lateness to work. A survey of 1,000 workers in the United Kingdom revealed that 23 percent of them reported being fired for things like doing personal tasks on lunch breaks, going to the bathroom too frequently, or being overly social. However, in a world driven by capitalism, professionalism is based on a monochronic relationship to timeliness and work style. It centers productivity over people, values time commitments, accomplishes tasks in a linear fashion, and often favors individuals who are white and Western. In contrast, polychronic cultures, while still able to get tasks completed, prioritize socialization and familial connections over economic labor. Within black and immigrant communities, there is often a deep ancestral connection to polychronic cultural orientation. Some people of color push against this by adopting a monochronic orientation, but many hold on to their polychronic work style. As a result, they may lose their jobs more often in a culture biased against their norms."

41 Janel George, "A Lesson on Critical Race Theory," American Bar Association, January 11, 2021, https://www.americanbar.

org/groups/crsj/publications/human_rights_magazine_home/civil-rights-reimagining-policing/a-lesson-on-critical-race-theory/

42 It's worth noting that Weems's *Life of Washington*, though wildly popular, was widely recognized as unreliable as soon as it appeared, with one contemporary reviewer calling it "eighty pages of as entertaining and edifying matter as can be found in the annals of fanaticism and absurdity." Katie Uva, "Parson Weems," George Washington's Mount Vernon, https://www.mountvernon.org/library/digitalhistory/digital-encyclopedia/article/parson-weems/

43 From the webinar "Perfecters of Democracy," September 15, 2020; quoted by *The Harvard Crimson*, https://www.thecrimson.com/article/2020/9/16/nikole-hannah-jones-radcliffe-talk/

44 Claretta Bellamy, "Nikole Hannah-Jones on the 1619 Project Book, Harsh Truths of the Black Experience," NBC News, November 18, 2021, https://www.nbcnews.com/news/nbcblk/nikole-hannah-jones-1619-project-book-harsh-truths-black-experience-rcna5876

45 "We Respond to the Historians Who Critiqued the 1619 Project," *The New York Times,* December 20, 2019, https://www.nytimes.com/2019/12/20/magazine/we-respond-to-the-historians-who-critiqued-the-1619-project.html

46 Leslie M. Harris, "I Helped Fact-Check the 1619 Project. The Times Ignored Me," *Politico,* March 6, 2020, https://www.politico.com/news/magazine/2020/03/06/1619-project-new-york-times-mistake-122248

47 For the full text of Nikole Hannah-Jones's lead essay for the 1619 Project, see: "America Wasn't a Democracy, Until Black Americans Made it One," *The New York Times,* August 14, 2019, https://www.nytimes.com/interactive/2019/08/14/magazine/black-history-american-democracy.html

48 "New York Times Quietly Edits '1619 Project' After Conservative Pushback," The Heritage Foundation, September 26, 2020, https://www.heritage.org/american-founders/impact/new-york-times-quietly-edits-1619-project-after-conservative-pushback

49 For a transcript of the key passage in the Somerset ruling, see Appendix 1, here: "Somerset's Case and its Antecedents in Imperial Perspective," The History Cooperative, 2006, https://web.archive.org/web/20070102150330/http://www.historycooperative.org/journals/lhr/24.3/cleve.html

50 For a detailed account of how underwhelming the English abolitionist cause remained during the decade of the 1770s, see Sean Wilentz's excellent dissection of Hannah-Jones's central claim in "A Matter of Facts," for *The Atlantic*, January 22, 2020: https://www.theatlantic.com/ideas/archive/2020/01/1619-project-new-york-times-wilentz/605152/

51 Andrew M. McCarthy, "What the Media Didn't Tell You about the Chauvin Case," National Review Online, April 24, 2021, https://www.nationalreview.com/2021/04/what-the-media-didnt-tell-you-about-the-chauvin-case/

52 *Ibid*

53 *Ibid*

54 Andrew M. McCarthy, "The DOJ's Civil-Rights Case in George Floyd's Killing: How Race Factors In," National Review Online, January 25, 2022, https://www.nationalreview.com/2022/01/the-dojs-civil-rights-case-in-george-floyds-killing-how-race-factors-in/

55 Roland Fryer, "An Empirical Analysis of Racial Differences in Police Use of Force," *Journal of Political Economy* 127, no. 3 (2016), https://scholar.harvard.edu/fryer/publications/empirical-analysis-racial-differences-police-use-force

56 Margaret Kimberley, "Freedom Rider: When Uncle Tom Fails," The Black Agenda Report, May 30, 2018, https://www.blackagendareport.com/freedom-rider-when-uncle-tom-falls

57 Devon W. Carbado, and Daria Roithmayr, "Critical Race Theory Meets Social Science," *Annual Review of Law and Social Science* 10, (November 2014). The abstract can be found online at: https://www.annualreviews.org/doi/abs/10.1146/annurev-lawsocsci-110413-030928#:~:text=Social%20science%20research%20offers%20critical,to%20support%20key%20empirical%20claims.

58 *Ibid*

59 John McWhorter, "The 'badass motherfucker' problem in the Black community," interview by Glenn Loury, The Glenn Show, April 27, 2021, https://glennloury.substack.com/p/the-badass-motherfucker-problem-in

60 *Ibid*

61 Massimo Calabresi, "Dispatches Skin Deep 101" *Time*, February 14, 1994, http://content.time.com/time/subscriber/article/0,33009,980105,00.html

62 Leonard Jeffries, "Our Sacred Mission," (text of Jeffries's original speech at the Empire State Black Arts and Cultural Festival in Albany, New York, July 20, 1991), https://www.linkedin.com/pulse/words-inspiration-our-sacred-mission-dr-leonard-jeffries-bomani/

63 *Ibid*

64 Jeff Sherry, "Ministry of Silly Walks," by Monty Python, YouTube, December 6, 2016, https://www.youtube.com/watch?v=eCLp7zodUiI

65 Lisa Lerer, and Sydney Ember, "Examining Tara Reade's Sexual Assault Allegation Against Joe Biden," *The New York Times,* April 12, 2020, https://www.nytimes.com/2020/04/12/us/politics/joe-biden-tara-reade-sexual-assault-complaint.html

66 Ryan Grim, "New Evidence Supporting Credibility of Tara Reade's Allegation Against Joe Biden Emerges," *The Intercept*, April 24, 2020, https://theintercept.com/2020/04/24/new-evidence-tara-reade-joe-biden/

67 Gregg Re, "NYT updates Kavanaugh 'bombshell' to note accuser doesn't recall alleged assault," Fox News, September 16, 2020, https://www.foxnews.com/politics/nyt-kavanaugh-bombshell-goes-bust-after-2020-dems-use-it-to-call-for-impeachment

68 Jack Crowe, "Blasey Ford's Lawyer Admits Client Wants 'Asterisk' Next to Kavanaugh's Name When He Rules on Roe," National Review, September 4, 2019, https://www.yahoo.com/video/blasey-ford-lawyer-admits-client-171246314.html

69 Jason Johnson's remarks on Brett Kavanaugh can be found at: https://www.mrctv.org/embed/543204

70 Anna Chu, "Three Years After Brett Kavanaugh's Confirmation, We're Still Searching for Truth and Justice," National Women's Law Center, October 7, 2021, https://nwlc.org/three-years-after-brett-kavanaughs-confirmation-were-still-searching-for-truth-and-justice/

71 Alexander Hamilton, "The Federalist Papers: No. 78," Yale Law School: Lillian Goldman Law Library, https://avalon.law.yale.edu/18th_century/fed78.asp

72 Domenico Montanaro, "Poll: More Believe Ford Than Kavanaugh, A Cultural Shift From 1991," National Public Radio, October 3, 2018, https://www.npr.org/2018/10/03/654054108/poll-more-believe-ford-than-kavanaugh-a-cultural-shift-from-1991

73 Jennifer Marchbank and Gayle Letherby, *Introduction to Gender: Social Science Perspectives,* second edition (London and New York: Routledge, 2014), 25

74 Transcript of the sketch "Mystico and Janet" can be found at MontyPython.net. "Mystico and Janet

– Flats Built by Hypnosis," https://montycasinos.com/montypython/scripts/mystico.php.html

75 Marchbank and Letherby, 29

76 Letter: "A Man's World," *New York Times,* July 23, 1995, https://www.nytimes.com/1995/07/23/books/l-a-man-s-world-407295.html

77 Sian Ferguson, "4 Reasons Demanding 'Objectivity' in Social Justice Debates Can Be Oppressive," Everyday Feminism, March 27, 2016, https://everydayfeminism.com/2016/03/objectivity-can-be-oppressive/

78 Alex-Quan Pham, "3 Reasons It's Irrational to Demand 'Rationalism' in Social Justice Activism," Everyday Feminism, March 25, 2016, https://everydayfeminism.com/2016/03/why-rationalism-is-irrational/

79 Abby Ohlheiser, "The woman behind 'Me Too' knew the power of the phrase when she created it—10 years ago," *The Washington Post,* October 19, 2017, https://www.washingtonpost.com/news/the-intersect/wp/2017/10/19/the-woman-behind-me-too-knew-the-power-of-the-phrase-when-she-created-it-10-years-ago/

80 Video of Seth MacFarlane hosting the Academy Awards (and joking about Harvey Weinstein's reputation). Payggg, "Seth MacFarlane jokes at Oscar nominations," YouTube, January 12, 2013, https://www.youtube.com/watch?v=yIXkEgeevw8

81 Video of Meryl Streep thanking Harvey Weinstein (and calling him "God") at the Academy Awards. AwardsShowNetwork, "Hope Springs Star Meryl Streep Wins Best Actress Motion Picture Drama – Golden Globes 2012," YouTube, March 14, 2012, https://www.youtube.com/watch?v=J6d-Or-SQLk

82 Video of the standing ovation given to Roman Polanski (in absentia) at the Academy Awards. Oscars, "Roman Polanski

winning the Oscar for Directing," YouTube, September 28, 2011, https://www.youtube.com/watch?v=PXnNOBj26lk

83 Elahe Izadi, "Louis C.K. responds to sexual misconduct allegations: 'These stories are true'" *The Washington Post,* November 10, 2017, https://www.washingtonpost.com/news/arts-and-entertainment/wp/2017/11/10/louis-c-k-these-stories-are-true/

84 Claire Voon, "Renowned Artist Chuck Close Under Fire for Alleged Sexual Misconduct," Hyperallergic, December 20, 2017, https://hyperallergic.com/418222/chuck-close-accused-sexual-misconduct/?fbclid=IwAR1wPfs7hCS9wuplyPcgeDLIno7DSkR0hRwqqZIrw8sZKjMp4oMbImuCCIM

85 *Ibid*

86 Melanie Baker, "New Bill Likely to Shift #MeToo Cases from Arbitration to Courts," February 22, 2022, JDSUPRA, https://www.jdsupra.com/legalnews/new-bill-likely-to-shift-metoo-cases-4692818/

87 Video of Senator Mazie Hirono. "Senator to men: Shut up and step up," CNN, September 19, 2018, https://www.cnn.com/videos/politics/2018/09/19/mazie-hirono-men-shut-up-kavanaugh-sexual-assault-vpx.cnn

88 Zoe Greenberg, "What Happens to #MeToo When a Feminist is the Accused?" *New York Times*, August 13, 2018, https://www.nytimes.com/2018/08/13/nyregion/sexual-harassment-nyu-female-professor.html

89 Avital Ronnell, "The Test Drive," video of lecture given October 5, 2006, https://www.youtube.com/watch?v=xVwoN2aLvL0&t=550s (see 9:10 and following)

90 *Ibid.* Greenberg, *NYT*

91 "Blaming the victim is apparently OK when the accused in a Title IX proceeding is a feminist literary theorist," *Leiter Reports: A Philosophy Blog,* June 2018, https://leiterreports.

typepad.com/blog/2018/06/blaming-the-victim-is-apparently-ok-when-the-accused-is-a-feminist-literary-theorist.html

92 Gayatri Spivak, translator's preface to *Of Grammatology*, by Jacques Derrida (Baltimore: Johns Hopkins University Press, 1974), *xliv*

93 Mauricio de Aguiar Martins, "A nonhuman primate model to study the immunological effects of feminizing hormone therapy in transgender women," National Institutes of Health, November 15, 2021, https://reporter.nih.gov/search/03JCZddjXkWD73Qoc9P0JA/project-details/10307630

94 Benjamin Solomon, "Identical Twins" explanation at the website for the National Human Genome Research Institute, updated August 11, 2022, https://www.genome.gov/genetics-glossary/identical-twins?fbclid=IwAR0-aNaP_AZvZowGIxv-Itcl J4rSXGO1CGxTMrmPz4qK8fK9M62qxUkpBeE#:~:text=Identical%20twins%20share%20all%20of,the%20same%20or%20different%20sexes

95 Nancy Coleman, "Transgender man gives birth to a boy" CNN, July 31, 2017, https://www.cnn.com/2017/07/31/health/trans-man-pregnancy-dad-trnd/index.html

96 Simon Hattenstone, "The dad who gave birth: 'Being pregnant doesn't change me being a trans man,'" The Guardian, April 20, 2019, https://www.theguardian.com/society/2019/apr/20/the-dad-who-gave-birth-pregnant-trans-freddy-mcconnell

97 Nara Schoenberg, "In a first for Illinois, transgender man who gave birth will be listed as the father on his baby's birth certificate," *Chicago Tribune,* January 14, 2020, https://www.chicagotribune.com/lifestyles/ct-life-first-transgender-birth-certificate-tt-01132020-20200114-qfbbf3dvufhppid5shjru6l5xu-story.html

98 Zara Hanawait, "Transgender Man Gives Birth to Healthy Baby, Talks Navigating Pregnancy as a Man," *Parents*, March 24, 2022,

https://www.parents.com/pregnancy/everything-pregnancy/transgender-man-gives-birth-to-healthy-baby-talks-navigating/

99 Marie Claire Dorking, "The dad who gave birth: 'I didn't know I could still get pregnant,'" Yahoo News, March 7, 2022, https://www.yahoo.com/entertainment/trans-man-how-i-coped-with-my-shock-pregnancy-150015720.html

100 Hannah Sparks, "Transgender man gives birth after 'Grindr one-night stand' while transitioning," *The New York Post,* January 6, 2022, https://nypost.com/2022/01/06/trans-man-gives-birth-after-grindr-one-night-stand/

101 Jessica Summers, "Transgender man who gave birth to his son criticizes medical staff for calling him 'mother' and claims that it's 'important' to STOP automatically linking pregnancy with being a woman," Daily Mail, December 22, 2021, https://www.dailymail.co.uk/femail/article-10335475/A-transgender-father-gave-birth-son-revealed-nurses-misgender-him.html

102 Gabrielle Sorto, "A Teacher Says He was Fired for Refusing to Use Male Pronouns for a Transgender Student," CNN, October 2, 2019, https://www.cnn.com/2019/10/02/us/virginia-teacher-says-wrongfully-fired-student-wrong-pronouns-trnd/index.html

103 "Gender and Health" reference page at the website for the World Health Organization, https://www.who.int/health-topics/gender#tab=tab_1

104 *Ibid*

105 "Statements by Officials of the U.S. Department of Health and Human Services Commemorating the First Openly Transgender Four-Star Officer and First Female Four-Star Admiral of the U.S. Public Health Service Commissioned Corps on October 19, 2021," HHS, October 19, 2021, https://www.hhs.gov/about/news/2021/10/19/statements-officials-us-department-health-and-human-services-commemorating-first-openly-transgender-four-star-officer-first-female-four-star-admiral.html

106 "Wikipedia: Manual of Style/Gender Identity," https://en.wikipedia.org/wiki/Wikipedia:Manual_of_Style/Gender_identity#:~:text=It%20was%20decided%20that%20that,were%20notable%20under%20that%20name.&text=An%20inconclusive%20discussion%20about%20gender%20fluidity%20and%20self%2Didentification

107 "Written in DNA—study reveals potential biological basis for transgender," Hudson Institute of Medical Research, October 3, 2018, https://hudson.org.au/latest-news/written-in-dna-study-reveals-potential-biological-basis-for-transgender/

108 Mads G. Henrickson, Julie Nordgaard, and Lennart Jansson, "Genetics of Schizophrenia: Overview of Methods, Findings and Limitations," *Frontiers in Human Neuroscience* 11 (June 22, 2017), https://www.frontiersin.org/articles/10.3389/fnhum.2017.00322/full

109 Matt Donnelly, "Oscar-Nominated 'Umbrella Academy' Start Elliot Page Announces He Is Transgender," *Variety*, December 1, 2020, https://variety.com/2020/film/news/elliot-page-transgender-ellen-page-juno-umbrella-academy-1234843023/

110 Erica Green, Katie Benner, and Robert Pear, "'Transgender' Could Be Defined Out of Existence Under Trump Administration," *The New York Times*, October 21, 2018, https://www.nytimes.com/2018/10/21/us/politics/transgender-trump-administration-sex-definition.html

111 Andrew Sullivan, "The Nature of Sex" *New York Mag*, February 1, 2019, https://nymag.com/intelligencer/2019/02/andrew-sullivan-the-nature-of-sex.html

112 "A backlash against gender ideology is starting in universities," Economist, June 5, 2021, https://www.economist.com/international/2021/06/05/a-backlash-against-gender-ideology-is-starting-in-universities

113 Abby Gardner, "Transgender-Comments Controversy," *Glamour,* January 3, 2022, https://www.glamour.com/story/a-complete-breakdown-of-the-jk-rowling-transgender-comments-controversy

114 Gabrielle Bellot, "How JK Rowling Betrayed the World She Created," *Literary Hub,* June 10, 2020, https://lithub.com/how-jk-rowling-betrayed-the-world-she-created/

115 *Ibid.*

116 Paulina Dedaj, "Emma Weyant: Second-place finisher in Lia Thomas' NCAA championship race won Olympic medal in 2021" *Fox News,* March 18, 2022, https://www.foxnews.com/sports/emma-weyant-olympic-medalist-lia-thomas-ncaa-championships

117 John Lohn, "A Look At the Numbers and Times: No Denying the Advantages of Lia Thomas," *Swimming World,* April 5, 2022, https://www.swimmingworldmagazine.com/news/a-look-at-the-numbers-and-times-no-denying-the-advantages-of-lia-thomas/

118 Dinette Wilford, "Transgender swimmer Lia Thomas loses to another trans swimmer," *The Toronto Sun,* January 10, 2022, https://torontosun.com/sports/other-sports/transgender-swimmer-lia-thomas-loses-to-another-trans-swimmer

119 Steven Rondina, "Transgender Fighter Fallon Fox Loses Via TKO to Ashlee Evans-Smith at CFA 12," *The Bleacher Report,* October 12, 2013, https://bleacherreport.com/articles/1808902-transgender-fighter-fallon-fox-loses-via-tko-to-ashlee-evans-smith-at-cfa12

120 Jon Pike, Emma Hilton, and Leslie Howe, "Male and Female Athletic Performance: Worlds Apart," *Quillette,* December 11, 2021, https://quillette.com/2021/12/11/male-and-female-athletic-performance/

121 Cyd Zeigler, "Hannah Mouncey says teammates pushed her away over locker room use," *Outsports,* August 28, 2020, https://

www.outsports.com/2020/8/28/21402020/hannah-mouncey-trans-athlete-handball-aflw-locker-room-five-rings-podcast

122 "20 U.S. Code § 1681 – Sex," Cornell Law School, https://www.law.cornell.edu/uscode/text/20/1681

123 Colin Binkley, "Biden Admin Extends Title IX Protections to Transgender Students for *Associated Press* via *PBS Newshour*, June 10, 2021, https://www.pbs.org/newshour/education/biden-admin-extends-title-ix-protections-to-transgender-students

124 Laura Italiano, "NAACP leader has pretended to be black for years: family," *The New York Post*, February 12, 2015, https://nypost.com/2015/06/12/naacp-leader-has-pretended-to-be-black-for-years-family/

125 "Statement on Race," American Anthropological Association, https://www.americananthro.org/ConnectWithAAA/Content.aspx?ItemNumber=2583

126 "AABA Statement on Race and Racism," American Association of Biological Anthropologists, https://physanth.org/about/position-statements/aapa-statement-race-and-racism-2019/

127 Robin Dembroff and Dee Payton, "Why We Shouldn't Compare Transracial to Transgender Identity," *Boston Review*, November 18, 2020, https://bostonreview.net/articles/robin-dembroff-dee-payton-breaking-analogy-between-race-and-gender/

128 Gerrard Kaonga, "Why Was The Babylon Bee Suspended by Twitter? CEO Seth Dillon Reacts to Ban," *Newsweek*, March 21, 2022, https://www.newsweek.com/babylon-bee-seth-dillon-twitter-ban-censorship-rachel-levine-trans-debate-1689870

129 Helen Pluckrose, "How French 'Intellectuals' Ruined the West: Postmodernism and its Impact, Explained," *Areo*, March 27, 2017, https://areomagazine.com/2017/03/27/how-french-intellectuals-ruined-the-west-postmodernism-and-its-impact-explained/ (Video of the event can be seen at

https://www.youtube.com/watch?v=a6EASuhefeI&t=591s. The chant begins at roughly the twenty-minute mark.)

130 "Law Students Shout Down Speakers, Sparking Freedom Of Speech Debate" MSNBC YouTube Channel, March 28, 2022, https://www.youtube.com/watch?v=SETxQfJD-RU&t=13s

131 Statement cited by the Harvard GSAS Christian Community on the website for Harvard University, "Shield and 'Veritas' History," https://hgscf.org/harvard-shield/

132 Rick Mullin, "Behind the scenes at the STEM-humanities culture war," *Chemical and Engineering News,* July 16, 2019, https://cen.acs.org/education/undergraduate-education/Behind-the-scenes-STEM-humanities-culture-war/97/i29

133 "Enrollment in Undergraduate Education" American Council on Education, https://www.equityinhighered.org/indicators/enrollment-in-undergraduate-education/undergraduate-majors/

134 Mark J. Perry, "Chart of the Day: Female Shares of BA Degrees by Major, 1971 to 2017," *American Enterprise Institute,* May 3, 2019, https://www.aei.org/carpe-diem/chart-of-the-day-female-shares-of-ba-degrees-by-major-1971-to-2017/

135 Gayatri Spivak, translator's preface to *Of Grammatology*, by Jacques Derrida (Baltimore: Johns Hopkins University Press, 1974), *xliv*

ACKNOWLEDGMENTS

Adam Bellow and David S. Bernstein of the Bombardier imprint at Post Hill Press contracted this book, and I'm indebted to them for their input at every stage of its writing, editing, and production. I am also grateful to my agent, Andy Ross, whose politics are often at odds with mine, but who is that rarest of literary men nowadays who does more than pay lip service to free thought; he champions it.

Finally, I want to acknowledge, though not by name (because they would no doubt be appalled, and because witness relocation programs cannot accommodate every request) my many interlocutors, virtual and meat-world, whose arguments have helped shape and sharpen the analyses contained herein.

ABOUT THE AUTHOR

Mark Goldblatt is the award-winning author of the middle grade novels *Twerp* and its sequel *Finding the Worm* (both from Random House), as well as a half dozen novels and nonfiction books for adults. He has been published in many popular and academic newspapers and magazines including the *New York Times*, the *Wall Street Journal*, the *New York Post, USA Today, Time, National Review, Reason, Commentary, Quillette,* the *Daily Caller*, the *American Spectator*, the *New York Observer, Philosophy Now*, the *Sewanee Theological Review*, and the *Chronicle of Higher Education*. He teaches developmental English and religious history at Fashion Institute of Technology of the State University of New York.

Printed in the USA
CPSIA information can be obtained
at www.ICGtesting.com
LVHW082141050823
754449LV00012B/301